Y0-CQL-467

ROBERT LOUIS STEVENSON

ROBERT
LOUIS STEVENSON

By ROSALINE MASSON

KENNIKAT PRESS
Port Washington, N. Y./London

ROBERT LOUIS STEVENSON

First published in 1914
Reissued in 1970 by Kennikat Press
Library of Congress Catalog Card No: 77-103204
SBN 8046-0841-5

Manufactured by Taylor Publishing Company   Dallas, Texas

CONTENTS

I DESIRE to express my indebtedness to Sir Sidney Colvin for kind personal advice and information given to me when I had undertaken to write this little Life, and for allowing me to quote from the *Letters of Robert Louis Stevenson,* edited by him.

My grateful thanks are due also to Lord Guthrie for his great kindness in reading the proofs of this book, and making various suggestions, now incorporated.

ROSALINE MASSON.

Edinburgh, 1914.

"I wonder exceedingly if I have done anything at all good ; and who can tell me ? and why should I wish to know ? In so little a while, I, and the English language, and the bones of my descendants, will have ceased to be a memory ! And yet—and yet—one would like to leave an image for a few years upon men's minds—for fun."

R. L. S.

ROBERT LOUIS STEVENSON

CHAPTER I

" SMOUT "

IT is, here to us in Edinburgh, all so much a matter of
yesterday! His voice still rings behind the grey stone
walls, in the glad, mad talk that puzzled and troubled
his elders. His slight form still haunts the country roads
between Edinburgh and the Pentlands, and shivers in the
east wind that cuts the mist veiling the city. Such a
little while ago he was here—his friends and intimates
are still actively with us—and he? Visitors come to us
from the other side of the world, the side that is new, and
we show them our city, and they waive aside Sir Walter
and David Hume, and nod kindly dismissal to Burns;
—yea, they glance with passing comprehension at our
Castle, as old as the hill it stands on, and, walking down
our High Street over the history of centuries, they con-
fess Edinburgh to them is the city that Stevenson lived
in. Why is it? It is a wonderful thing when we remember that it is only twenty years since he died, and
less than forty since he began to write. What is his
fascination—what is his appeal? Genius we are
familiar with in Edinburgh, and with genius that compels
personal admiration we are not unfamiliar. But with
genius that inspires love? For his readers to-day love
Stevenson.

The parents of Robert Louis Stevenson were young
Edinburgh people. His father, Thomas Stevenson, had
been born and brought up in Edinburgh, one of the
thirteen children of the famous engineer of the Bell Rock
Lighthouse, Robert Stevenson. It is with this Robert
Stevenson, Robert Louis Stevenson's grandfather, that Sir
Walter Scott went the voyage in 1814, with the Light-

house Commissioners, that gave him his material for *The Pirate*, and of him Sir Walter records in his diary : " The official chief of the expedition is Mr. Stevenson, the surveyor—viceroy on the commission—a most gentlemanlike and modest man, and well known by his scientific skill."

While the youngest of this Robert Stevenson's sons, Thomas, was growing up, Robert Stevenson lived at No. 1 Baxter's Place, a big house with a long garden, with orchard and apple loft, at the foot of Calton Hill. Thomas was taught at a school near his home in Nelson Street, and then at the famous High School of Edinburgh —first at its Old Town site of many memories, and afterwards at its fine new home on the Calton Hill. When he was seventeen he was bound apprentice in his father's office, to be bred an engineer, and when he was twentyeight, in 1846, he was made a partner in the firm. In 1848, when thirty years of age, he married Margaret Isabella Balfour, the beautiful youngest daughter of the minister of Colinton—a picturesque village near Edinburgh—and the great-granddaughter of James Balfour, Professor of Moral Philosophy at Edinburgh University.[1]

The young people settled at 8 Howard Place, a substantial little two-storeyed stone house in a row on the northern slope of Edinburgh, leading down towards the Firth of Forth ; and here, on the 13th of November 1850, their son was born. The grit of Edinburgh—the dust of her historic stones—was in his blood. The first world the baby eyes rested on, uncomprehendingly, was the world of firelit murk of an Edinburgh November.

Three months before his birth, on 12th July 1850, his grandfather, Robert Stevenson, had died, and Edinburgh had lost a citizen who was an eminent worker, one of the originators of the Royal Observatory at Edinburgh, a Fellow of the Royal Society of Edinburgh and of the Antiquarian Society there, and a Fellow of the Geological Society and of the Astronomical Society of London. He was buried in the Calton Cemetery of Edinburgh, where lie so many of Edinburgh's notabilities ; and a copy of

[1] In this same year he became a Fellow of the Royal Society of Edinburgh, of which he was elected President in 1885.

his marble bust, the original of which is in the Bell Rock Lighthouse he reared, stands in the Museum of Science and Art in Edinburgh. Thomas Stevenson must undoubtedly have been very proud of his father, and proud of the tradition he left behind him. His death occurred in July, and little Louis, born four months later, came into existence at a sad time of his father's life ; and from the beginning Thomas Stevenson probably felt that the little son had come to carry on the name and the tradition, and the family work of ringing round with lights the wild, dangerous Scottish coasts.

The baby was, when a few days old, given the grandfather's Christian name, Robert. The ceremony took place, Scottish fashion, in the house. His other grandfather, the minister from Colinton, performed the ceremony, and the child was christened Robert Lewis Balfour.[1]

In January 1853 his parents moved to another, rather larger, house on the opposite side of the street ; and in the same year Thomas Stevenson and his brother David were appointed engineers to the Board of Northern Lighthouses.

The new house was No. 1 Inverleith Terrace, and the outgoing tenants in January 1853 were young Professor and Mrs. Aytoun—he, William Edmondstoune Aytoun, Professor of English Literature at Edinburgh University, one of the brilliant Blackwood coterie of that day, and afterwards author of *Lays of the Cavaliers* ; she, the daughter of Professor Wilson, " Christopher North." Witty Professor Aytoun, writing to an intimate friend, excuses himself for the extravagance of purchasing a house " big enough to lodge a patriarch " in Great Stuart Street, by complaints of 1 Inverleith Terrace— " there was a certain white silk dress, which recalls indistinct reminiscences of the altar, hanging peacefully on a peg. Blight and mildew ! It was spotted like a leopard's skin."

Until this time, the Stevensons' little son had been a healthy baby, " a fractious little fellow . . . decidedly

[1] When he was eighteen he dropped the " Balfour " and changed the spelling, though not the pronunciation, of " Lewis."

pretty, with dark eyes and fair hair," [1] toddling and climbing about, and learning quickly to speak. But his mother was delicate, with a tendency to chest weakness and nervous troubles. What a house to which to take a delicate wife and a little two-year-old ! Why, the house has three outside walls and faces the north, and evidently it was damp ! The first thing that happened was that the new tenants' baby had a severe attack of croup ; and from then onwards every year brought its attack of some illness, weakening the little frame. But the cold damp house remained their home for four years—just the same length of time the young Aytouns had endured it. It was here that Stevenson became an " eminently religious " child, as befitted the son of a father of Calvinistic leanings, and a grandson of the Manse. And here he learned by heart hymns and large passages of Scripture ; and after he was in bed he used to be overheard crooning " songstries "—and here, on 23rd April 1857, his father stood outside his door and took down the following " curious rambling effusion " :

> " Had not an angel got the pride of man,
>   No evil thought, no hardened heart would have been seen.
>   No hell to go to, but a heaven so pure ;
>   That angel was the Devil.
>   Had not that angel got the pride, there would have been no need
>   For Jesus Christ to die upon the cross."

Little, crooning, sleepless, seven-year-old denizen of the world—what did he know of evil thoughts and hardened hearts ! What in Heaven's name had he to do with hell and the Devil !

Next month, May 1857, the Stevensons again "flitted," the flitting this time marking an increase of prosperity. Better still, the new house, 17 Heriot Row, was wisely chosen, for Heriot Row is sunny and open, faces the south, and looks on to the lawns and trees of the gardens that fill the sloping space between it and sombre Queen Street, facing down northward above it.

This house, 17 Heriot Row, was the Stevensons' home for the rest of their days.

---

[1] Mrs. Sellar's *Recollections and Impressions.*

It was in this year, his eighth year, the year in which
they moved to Heriot Row, that little " Smout," as his
doting parents called him, " learnt to read easily to himself." But " Smout " was already an author—had he
not, in his sixth year, before he could read or write,
dictated a " History of Moses " to a devoted scribe ? And
little " Smout," alas ! was already something else. He
was already a very often ailing little boy, with weak
digestion and weak chest ; and in the autumn of the
year after his parents moved with him to Heriot Row—
the autumn of 1858—he nearly died of gastric fever.

Louis Stevenson in after life used to like saying he
had had a " Covenanting childhood." Certainly the
gloom of Calvinism hung about him in his infancy.
Thomas Stevenson, little Louis's father, was a man of
brilliant scientific faculty, strongly religious, grave and
upright, full of strong, honest, Scottish prejudices.

" Left to himself," one of their early friends relates, " life was
' full of sairiousness ' to him ; and had it not been for his strong
sense of humour, which was a striking trait in his character, the
Calvinism in which he had been brought up would have left its
gloomy mark upon him. Among the pictures on the wall " (at
their first house, Howard Place) " was a fine engraving of David
Hume, whose writings, in spite of his opinions, he greatly
admired ; ' but,' he said, ' I shall take that down when the boy
is old enough to notice it, for I should not like him to think
Hume was one of my heroes.' " [1]

Mrs. Stevenson, a daughter of the Manse, thoroughly
sincere in her religion, had less depth of religious feeling.
She was cheerful and vivacious and " sweet as sugar,"
another old friend testifies. But even the lighter-hearted
mother was reduced to the pious fraud of setting a pack
on to a toy wooden figure so that it might represent
Christian with his burden, and making her little sickly
child promise to play at nothing more secular than
" Pilgrim's Progress " before she would let him have his
toys on Sunday.

And " Cummie," his faithful and devoted nurse, whose

[1] Mrs. Sellar's *Recollections and Impressions.* The remark about
Hume will be recognised by those who knew Thomas Stevenson
as one of his characteristic jests.

name is now known wherever Stevenson is read, was
even more devout. She taught her little charge his
Bible and his Shorter Catechism, and steeped his little
receptive mind in all the doctrines of her faith.

Another element of his "Covenanting childhood"
cannot be ignored: the thrilling tales in missionary travels
and books of martyrology and history, like *The Scottish
Worthies*, *Fox's Book of Martyrs*, &c., which were in
every middle-class Scottish household, and were read
every Sunday by young and old.

Stevenson himself sets no small value on the effect of
such Sabbaths on Scottish character. "Sabbath ob-
servance," he assures us,[1]

"makes a series of grim and perhaps serviceable pauses in the
tenor of Scottish boyhood—days of great stillness and solitude
for the rebellious mind, when in the dearth of books and play,
and in the intervals of studying the Shorter Catechism, the
intellect and senses prey upon and test each other. The typical
English Sunday, with the huge midday dinner and the plethoric
afternoon, leads perhaps to different results. About the very
cradle of the Scot there grows up a hum of metaphysical
divinity; and the whole of two divergent systems is summed
up, not merely speciously, in the first two questions of the rival
catechisms, the English tritely inquiring, ' What is your name ?'
the Scottish striking at the very root of life with, ' What is the
chief end of man ?' and answering nobly if obscurely, 'To glorify
God and to enjoy him for ever."

It was all perfectly natural in the Edinburgh of half a
century ago—more than half the little boys who then
lived in the nurseries on the top storeys of our well-to-do
houses, and who trudged backwards and forwards
through the dreary streets between their homes and the
Academy, then as now—more than half these promising
little urchins were being brought up in the same fashion.
And many a man now, prosperous and professional,
golfing on Sundays, spoiling his own children, can recall
exactly such Sabbaths, such walks, such teachings, and
such wholesome personal terror of his Satanic Majesty.

But, if the winds of Edinburgh chill the bones, Edin-

[1] "The Foreigner at Home," in *Memories and Portraits*.

burgh has many days of sunshine. Was there ever such
love, such tenderness, such idolatry, as were lavished on
little Louis Stevenson ? His mother in her diary fondly
chronicled his doings and quoted his childish little say-
ings ; his father stood outside the door to listen and take
down his rhythmic croonings ; and the same Cummie
who taught him the Shorter Catechism, in the long nights
when the poor little man lay awake and racked with
coughing and prayed " for sleep or morning "—faithful
Cummie used to lift him out of bed and carry him to the
window, and show him one or two lit-up windows in the
dark line of Queen Street above them through the trees
of the gardens between, and they would tell one another
" there might be sick little boys and their nurses waiting
like us for the morning." " She was more patient than
I can suppose an angel," he records. When the nights
were worse, and led to feverish sleep broken by delirium
and wild imaginative terrors, then his kind, gentle father
would come up and soothe him, holding feigned conver-
sations to amuse and interest the boy, till he quieted
him down. And " joy came back with the day " that
was heralded by the creaking wheels of the first of the
train of carts coming in from the country in the dark
of the winter's morning.

Probably the happiest times of his childhood were in
summer, for in summer he was fairly well, and most of
the summers were spent in country places near Edinburgh. His grandfather's Manse at Colinton played an
important part in his childhood. Always a glamour
hung on his memory of that Manse : " That was my
golden age : *et ego in Arcadia vixi.*" The joy it must
have been to the solitary little boy to be fetched by the
old family phaeton, and driven through the familiar
streets of his daily walks, and out into the country, and
to all the delights of the grandfather's Manse ! Of his
grandfather himself he stood in wholesome awe ; but
the dignified old gentleman, who usually held himself
in scholarly and ministerial aloofness from the life of
the house, must have been very kind to his youngest
daughter's delicate little child. Stevenson remembers

once exhibiting, by request, a box of tin soldiers, and marshalling his armies on the mahogany table after dinner, while the stately grandfather cracked his nuts and sipped his port.

The presiding genius of the Manse was Miss Jane Balfour, Mrs. Stevenson's unmarried sister, warm and kind of heart, who not only kept her father's house, but mothered all her little nephews and nieces. Occasionally as many as half a score of them at a time overran the Manse—chiefly sallow little people from India, when their own parents could not take care of them. Aunt Jane, "Chief of Aunts," had been a wit and a beauty—a "wilful empress"—in her youth; but a riding accident had left her "nearly deaf and blind," and had turned her, as Stevenson remarks with all the unconscious selfishness of man, into "the most serviceable of women."

Here at the Manse was the "long low dining-room" connected in his mind with daylight games of "tig," and of nights when, after dinner, the shaded lamp was lit, and the aunt sat down to read in the rocking chair, and for the imaginative little boy guest "there was a great open space behind the sofa left entirely in the shadow" where he could crawl about stealthily, peering out at the unconscious people in the circle of lamplight, and weaving fancies and imaginary adventures. Then there was the storeroom, where his aunt used to take the little weakling in the forenoon and give him three Albert biscuits and some calf-foot jelly : "that storeroom was a most voluptuous place with its piles of biscuit boxes and spice tins, the rack for buttered eggs, the little window that let in sunshine and the flickering shadow of leaves, and the strong sweet odour of everything that pleaseth the taste of man."

And the out-of-door life at Colinton ! "The sloping lawn that was literally steeped in sunshine," the stable and coach-house, the river between its steep banks, and the kirkyard "about which we were always hovering at even with the strange attraction of fear." To the little band of nephews and nieces at the Manse, all these were a world of romantic possibilities for play and "make-believe." What matter if the Manse lay down in a hollow beside the river and below the kirkyard—" the black slow water," the " strange wet smell," the " draggled vegetation on the far side whither the current took everything," were all fondly remembered as part of the Arcadia ;—and so were the " spunkies " who, undoubtedly playing among the graves, were eagerly watched for from the Manse windows after nightfall. Better all this, in spite of the damp, than those dreary walks he and Cummie took together.

But Colinton was not the furthest extent of his " ken." When he was only seven he was taken over the Border for the first time, and stayed with his parents at the English Lakes. Holidays played an important part in the life of little " Smout." But life, even at nine years old, cannot be all holidays.

If Stevenson had lived in the days of the various " Who's Who " publications, he would have been obliged to enter, under " education," " Edinburgh Academy and University " ;—but he would have smiled, with his pen poised, before he did so. It would not have been true in spirit, whatever it would have been in letter. For Stevenson's " education " was a series of snapped threads. When he was barely seven, in the first autumn at Heriot Row, he had been sent to a preparatory school kept by a Mr. Henderson, in India Street, a street leading out of Heriot Row ; but he went only for a few weeks. Two years later, in October 1859, he was sent back to the same school, and attended it until, at the age of eleven, he began an intermittent attendance at the Academy, which lasted until he was fourteen. The discipline on which schoolmasters insist nowadays, on the all-important matter of little boys' schooling, and which falls heaviest on parents and sisters, seems either not to have been enforced then, or else Mr. and Mrs. Stevenson did not submit to it. When Stevenson's parents wanted to travel, they travelled ; and they took Smout with them.

In 1862, when he was twelve, they went to London and to the south of England, for the sake of Mr. Stevenson's health. In July of the same year they took the boy to Hamburg. The whole of the next year was spent in travel—it was now Mrs. Stevenson's health that in January took them all to Mentone for three months, after which they went a magnificent tour, taking the boy with them, visiting Genoa, Naples, Rome, Florence, and Venice, and returning down the Rhine. After this tour the mother remained in England, and " Smout," much travelled and experienced, was allowed to return alone from London to Edinburgh, which he reached on 29th May, when the worst of the east winds might be supposed to be over, and the sun was probably shining on the castled town. The Academy, which could never have seen much of him, was to see him no more.

That autumn the boy accompanied his father on a tour of inspection of the lighthouses of Fife ; and on their return, Mr. and Mrs. Stevenson, again for the sake of Mrs. Stevenson's health, went back to Mentone—and this time the boy was not taken. " Aunt Jane," the " Chief of Aunts," was now living at Spring Grove, near London, in charge of some of her nephews, Louis's cousins, who attended a school there ; and to this school little Louis was sent as a boarder for one winter term. But in spite of being allowed to visit his aunt's house, he was not happy—is it likely, after Naples, Rome, Florence, Venice, and London, that he would be ?

He found his English schoolfellows uncongenial. They were fond of games, and Stevenson was not. This in itself would, in an English school, have made him feel an alien. And they were unimaginative, and young for their age. Stevenson was never young till he grew up.

The day before his thirteenth birthday he wrote his mother a letter that began in dog-French and ended : " My dear Papa, you told me to tell you whenever I was miserable. I do not feel well, and I wish to get home. Do take me with you." The appeal must have prevailed, for Thomas Stevenson came and fetched " Smout " from Mr. Wyatt's school, and he spent Christmas with his parents on the French Riviera, and they remained there till May 1864.

His next school, which he attended irregularly from
1864 till 1867, was a private school for delicate or back-
ward boys, kept by a Mr. Thompson, in Frederick Street,
Edinburgh.

Here his classmates numbered about a dozen, aged
from nine to fifteen, and there were no home lessons.
But even this school discipline was broken ; for during
these years Louis was taken away from Edinburgh a
good deal, either for the sake of his parents' healths, or
for the sake of his own. Many of the journeys were not
far journeys—Bridge of Allan, Dunoon, Rothesay,
North Berwick, Lasswade, and Peebles—but the springs
of 1865 and 1866 the mother and son spent at Torquay.
During these times away from school, Louis received
teaching from various tutors. At Peebles in 1864, for
instance, he had lessons with the master of the Burgh
School, who reported him as the most intelligent and
best-informed boy he had ever known—no doubt true !
At Mentone he had French lessons, which were apparently delightful to master and pupil alike, for they de-
veloped into talk in French, and lessons in piquet and
card tricks. In Torquay in 1865 he began German with
a private tutor. It was all very desultory, and it had
the effect that unsystematic training, combined with
much freedom and constant grown-up society, naturally
has on a clever child ;—the boy grew up precocious, interesting, affected, and egregiously egotistic. Moreover,
an only child of devoted parents, in missing systematic
training, he missed none of the selfishness that systematic training encourages. And here his character might
have ended had Louis Stevenson possessed no powers
beyond those he showed as a clever, spoilt, sensitive,
troublesome boy, and had his destiny shaped itself as
must then have seemed most probable, and landed him
in an engineer's office, or gifted him with a wig and gown
and a brass plate, and added yet another prosperous
citizen and dinner-table wit to the ranks of Edinburgh
society. But Fate and those about him were trying to
mould a creature who possessed that unmouldable and
rare and incalculable quality we call " genius." And

the boy Stevenson—"long, lean, and spidery," flat-chested, and with the oval face and soft brown eyes familiar to everyone to-day—had already other ideals than those held up before him. The brown eyes already mocked the world, and the fingers were already inky.

Without doubt the upright, kind-hearted father must often, as the long limbs grew longer, have looked anxiously at this strange being who was his only son; yet he was ever proud of him, and ready to be sympathetic. Stevenson's earliest efforts at literary production had taken the form familiar to every household—MS. magazines. "The Schoolboys' Magazine," edited when he was thirteen, he filled with the usual schoolboy adventures, lurid with horrors and destitute of heroines—save for that interjected detail which so amused Stevenson himself in after years : "But I forgot to tell you that I had made love to a beautiful girl even in one day, and from all I knew she loved me." "The Sunbeam Magazine" was a more mature effort, to which he contributed when he was sixteen, and came after an attempt at novel writing begun when he was fifteen. At this time too he embarked on another story, founded on "The Pentland Rising", a Covenanting episode. The subject-matter of this must have been as congenial to the father as to the boy ; and to the writing of it young Stevenson brought all the Covenanting enthusiasm learned at his nurse's knee, and all his familiar knowledge of the scenery of the Pentlands and Colinton. But he made of it a story, and Mr. Stevenson thought this spoilt it. They must have talked it over together ; and Louis Stevenson, at Heriot Row, in the last months of his fifteenth year, altered his story to please his father, and before that year 1866 was over, his first printed work was published by Andrew Elliot in Edinburgh—a small anonymous green pamphlet called "The Pentland Rising : a Page of History, 1666." And most of the copies of the small edition were bought by his father.

And now "Smout" was no more.

CHAPTER II

" VELVET COAT "

IN May 1867, when Louis Stevenson was in his seventeenth year, his parents rented " Little Swanston," a stone cottage set in an old-fashioned garden on a hillside about three miles from Edinburgh, within half-an-hour's walk of the outskirts of the town, and within less than that distance from Colinton, Mrs. Stevenson's birthplace, with its old Manse of past memories.

All the country round it must have been familiar to the boy, and no doubt the taking of Swanston, like so many acts of his parents, was—in the old phrase—to do their son pleasure. But also one likes to think that the kind, patient father foresaw, in taking this sheltered and accessible cottage for a country residence, that it would lead to more cheerful summers than those he had grown to dread, when his wife and son had to go for their healths to the South, and leave him alone in Edinburgh. Those must have been dreary times for Mr. Stevenson, himself not strong, when he lived alone for weeks together in the Heriot Row house, going daily to his office, and returning to lonely meals. He had, of course, many friends in Edinburgh, and was universally popular with them ; but Edinburgh is not social in spring and summer, for in spring the east wind dries the air and nips the blood, and luxurious people, when the " Courts rise," go abroad ; and Mr. Stevenson may well have found even the Clubs half deserted. And in summer all the houses are left empty, the long rows of windows in the grey stone crescents and terraces are filled with brown paper, and the grass grows up unrebuked between the cobbles on the roads.

When the Stevensons first went to it, Swanston Cottage was very small indeed ; but there was one spare room, and the anxious parents were glad of that, for Louis Stevenson could put up a friend, not only in the summer, when they were in residence, but at any time he chose to go out there.

All the ground round about Swanston is historic.

Close below Swanston was, it is asserted, the site of a Roman town ; and there are still traces of the conquering race of the old world in a little Roman bridge with a " skewed arch " over the Powburn, and in a great unhewn battle-stone, standing huge and awesome and lonely in a field, among grass or furrows or turnips, as the case may be, and telling to ears that hear not of a battle fought between the Picts and the Romans, watched by the selfsame hills. And on these hills, centuries later, the Covenanters, beloved by Louis Stevenson, marched and sang, and encamped before the battle of Rullion Green.

There are two ways to Swanston from Edinburgh. There is the road leading straight out south from the suburb of Morningside, and turning sharply at Fairmilehead ; and there is the road from the north-west that, leading from the main road out to Colinton, climbs steeply up from Craiglockhart to Fairmilehead.

Often must young Stevenson have come up this road past " Hunter's Tryst," where, it is said, Allan Ramsay laid the scenery of *The Gentle Shepherd*, and where, in the little roadside inn which Sir Walter Scott and the Ettrick Shepherd knew so well, the ". Six Foot Club " used to meet and make very merry. The quiet cart-road to Swanston turns out of this road a few steps past the sharp turn at Hunter's Tryst, and before it reaches the crossroads of Fairmilehead. It leads straight up to the hills—to the green slopes of Allermuir, one of the Pentland range—a gentle ascent between fields, and across the tiny trickling burn fringed with willows. It is all now as it was in Stevenson's day—the big open cart-shed at the roadside, with its upturned carts belonging to " Big Swanston," or " Jack's Farm "—the hens scraping and picking about among the shafts—and then the farm itself, once a Grange belonging to a religious house, and a fine old stone building still, with gabled side and " crow steps." The road ends with the farm, and never reveals the secret that, hidden behind, is one of the prettiest and most picturesque of villages, thatched and " harled," set round about a village green and a burn. Swanston Cottage itself stands in a cup in the slope of the hill, and, in its leafy garden, remains almost hidden, save for its

chimneys. It was built by the Edinburgh magistrates
as a retreat for themselves on their own ground—for the
burn at Swanston, after the middle of the eighteenth
century, used to supply the town with water, and the
ground belonged to the " Corporation," and the magistrates had to drive out and inspect the waterworks.
These wise magistrates built it sheltered by a knoll from
the winds off the sea, with its back turned to the
north and to Edinburgh, and its bow-windows at the
front looking straight south and to the hills ; and they
laid out a gerden and planted it with trees, and brought
crockets and gargoyles from poor long-suffering St. Giles's
Church, which they were " restoring " (oh shade of Gavin
Douglas !), and used them to ornament their doorway and
gables and garden.

This, then, was the country home leased by Mr.
Stevenson in 1867, where, for the next fourteen years,
they lived constantly from March to October—the
" kintry hame " Louis Stevenson so loved, and remembered so tenderly and intimately that he could, writing
years afterwards in the Tropics, describe it all from
memory in almost the last romance he wrote, and in
his passionately homesick poems.

After the first summer at Swanston, in November 1867,
Louis Stevenson entered Edinburgh University, and
took out the Latin and Greek classes—Professor Sellar's
and Professor Blackie's. The Stevensons were back by
now in their own house in Heriot Row, where the two
rooms that had been Smout's nurseries had long since
been turned into his bedroom and sitting-room—the
sitting-room or " study " to the back, with, from its
window, a view over chimneys and roofs to the Forth
and the Fife hills beyond, and on its walls a quaint
assortment of all young Stevenson's favourite books.

If the boy was a systematic truant from his classes at
the University, his father was the last to blame him.
How could he ? Mr. Stevenson had in his own boyhood
been himself a " consistent idler " as regarded regular
schooling, and on principle had never asked Louis, all his
intermittent schooldays, how he stood in his classes. It
is told that Mr. Stevenson used to stop small boys in the

street, and, examining their little straps of books, earnestly advise them not to trouble their heads with the " rubbish that was being crammed into them," but to read what they felt inclined to read, and to play to their hearts' content. The little open-mouthed boys in the street probably merely thought the gentleman mad; but young Louis at home not only understood and appreciated his father's educational theories, but put them into practice, and assiduously read what he felt inclined to read, and played to his heart's content. At the end of his first session at the University, when he presented himself before Professor Blackie and asked for a certificate of attendance, Professor Blackie, looking with his shrewd blue eyes at the singular youth before him, remarked with unconscious sarcasm, " I do not know your face." But he gave him his certificate all the same. " But although I am the holder of a certificate in the Professor's own hand," wrote Stevenson in *The New Amphion* many a long year after, " I cannot remember to have been present in the Greek class above a dozen times."

All this time Mr. Stevenson was not without his own ambition for his only son—an ambition as deep-rooted in his pride as the ambition of any father who has received a great inheritance, and treasured it and bettered it to hand on to his son. The inheritance of the Stevensons was their great business of official engineers to the Commissioners of the Northern Lights. It was, in Thomas Stevenson's mind, as much ordained that Robert Louis Stevenson should be a civil engineer, as had been his father and his grandfather before him, and should continue their splendid work of lighting the wild Scottish coasts, as it is ordained in the mind of any great landowner with a historic name that the little son at his side shall one day inherit the acres and the titles, the traditions and responsibilities. This man's regard for his son is always unconsciously aware of this; and so it must have been with Thomas Stevenson.

In the second summer of Louis's University days, the summer of 1868, when he was seventeen, the "summer excursions took a professional turn," and the boy went in July to Anstruther in Fife, and in August and the first

half of September to Wick, to watch the works of the
firm. What was the result ? Stevenson wrote to his
father from Anstruther :

" It is awful how slowly I draw, and how ill . . . when I'm
drawing I find out something I have not measured, or having
measured, have not noted, or, having noted, cannot find." [1]

A later letter to his mother ends :

" I am utterly sick of this grey, grim, sea-beaten hole. I
have a little cold in my head, which makes my eyes sore ; and
you can't tell how utterly sick I am, and how anxious to get
back among trees and flowers and something less meaningless
than this bleak fertility. Papa need not imagine that I have a
bad cold or am stone blind from this description, which is the
whole truth . . . I should like to cut the business and come
right slick out to Swanston. . . ." [1]

It would be a perfectly natural but an altogether unsympathetic judgment to say that Stevenson was at this
time a spoilt boy, visiting upon his parents all his little
ailments and feelings, " sparing them nothing," and trying to get his own way. It would perhaps be truer to
think of him as beginning to show the irresponsible traits
that go with that quality we call genius, and that make
genius a trying housemate. You can no more expect
a genius to conform to other people's standards than you
can expect to saddle and bridle an eagle.

His letters the next month from Wick must have delighted his father's heart, especially the account of
" roughing it," and the description of his watching a
great storm—waves twenty feet high and spray rising
eighty feet—and of his standing looking at the sea and
listening to its monotonous roar and the shriek of the
wind, and remembering the verse :

> " But yet the Lord that is on high
> Is more of might by far
> Than noise of many waters is
> Or great sea billows are."

Stevenson the father would no doubt readily have for-
given wild Wick for being his only failure—for the sea at

[1] *Letters of Robert Louis Stevenson* (edited by Sir Sidney Colvin).

Wick proved too strong for the work of man, and the harbour had to be abandoned—had it made a man and an engineer of young Louis. But he was neither—he was a freak and a poet.

The next winter in Edinburgh Stevenson again attended the Latin class, but Professor Blackie and Greek were given up as hopeless. It was during this, his second winter at college, that a meeting took place that led to his making one of the few congenial family friendships of his own social standing that Stevenson enjoyed in Edinburgh. Professor Jenkin (whose life Stevenson was afterwards to write) was in 1868 appointed to the Chair of Engineering at Edinburgh University. No doubt Mrs. Stevenson, Edinburgh fashion, punctiliously paid her call of welcome on the wife of the new Professor soon after their arrival, and when Mrs. Jenkin, late one afternoon in the winter of that year, paid her first call on Mrs. Stevenson in Heriot Row, it was probably a "return call." She and her hostess sat talking by the firelight, and the conversation may have begun on conventional lines, and Mrs. Jenkin been asked if she liked Edinburgh. But the talk was interrupted. The incident must be told in Mrs. Jenkin's own inimitable words :

"Suddenly, from out of a dark corner beyond the fireplace, came a voice, peculiar, vibrating : a boy's voice, I thought at first. 'Oh !' said Mrs. Stevenson, 'I forgot that my son was in the room. Let me introduce him to you.' The voice went on : I listened in perplexity and amazement. Who was this son who talked as Charles Lamb wrote ? this young Heine with a Scottish accent ? I stayed long, and when I came away the unseen converser came down with me to the front door to let me out. As he opened it, the light of the gas-lamp outside ('For we are very lucky, with a lamp before the door,' he sings) fell on him, and I saw a slender, brown, long-haired lad, with great dark eyes, a brilliant smile, and a gentle, deprecating bend of the head. 'A boy of sixteen,' I said to myself. But he was eighteen, looking then, as he always did, younger than his age. I asked him to come and see us. He said, 'Shall I come to-morrow ?' I said 'Yes,' and ran home. As I sat down to dinner I announced, 'I have made the acquaintance of a poet !' He came on the morrow, and from that day forward we saw him constantly. From that day forward, too, our affection and our admiration for him, and our delight in his company, grew."

This is the woman's point of view. We have the man's point of view in this description of Louis Stevenson in his student days by one who had been a fellow-student :

" A thin pale-faced youth," the writer calls Stevenson, " with piercing eyes, ever in a hurry, cigarette in mouth and muffler round his neck, and with loose locks which suggested an advisable early interview with a skilful barber." [1]

Stevenson himself describes, with deeply sympathetic insight, his student looks and his student self :

" A certain lean, ugly, idle, unpopular student, full of changing humours, fine occasional purposes of good, unflinching acceptance of evil, shiverings on wet east-windy mornings, journeys up to class, infinite yawnings during lectures, and unquestionable gusto in the delights of truantry." [2]

It is in that " unflinching acceptance of evil " that we get the key to all Stevenson's strength and all his weakness. What was the evil that had to be accepted in the life of this only son, who seemed to have so happy a fate prepared for him by indulgent hands ? Had he not everything given him that his parents could provide ?—the comfortable, cheerful home in Heriot Row, with his own study sacred to his whims and his leisure ; the life of his elders made, unconsciously to both in great measure, subservient to him ; the ready hospitality to all his respectable intimates ; the " young dinners " ; the anxious inducements offered to him to make friends among his own rank and caste ; the little cottage nestling on the hills and facing the sun, where he could go at any time and be host and idler ? How many of his Scottish fellow-students, comparing his life and opportunities with theirs, must have looked on him as a pampered child of fortune ! And yet, recalling his student days, " unflinching acceptance of evil," he wrote. It was that subtlest form of all evils he had to accept, the war of temperament against environment. Louis Stevenson was abnormal, both in mind and body. He was an invalid, trying to live the life of ordinary youth in a climate that is not

[1] Quoted in *R. L. Stevenson's Edinburgh Days*, by Eve Blantyre Simpson.

[2] *Some College Memories*, by R. L. Stevenson, in *The New Amphion*. (Privately printed.)

adapted for invalids ; and he was a genius, trying to feel
his way in a world that is not adapted to geniuses,
because it is ruled by laws and customs made for, and
made by, very average intellects. Already Stevenson was
assailed by " many perplexities," and " began to per-
ceive that life was a handicap upon strange, wrong-sided
principles; and not, as he had been told, a fair and equal
race." It is generally those who are unfairly handicapped who cry out against the injustice of life : with
Stevenson it was otherwise : his mind was unsettled at
Edinburgh University—where, under the democratic
Scottish system, " all classes rub shoulders on the greasy
benches. The raffish young gentleman in gloves must
measure his scholarship with the plain, clever, clownish
laddie from the Parish School "—by the comparison of
his own conditions—the son of a man in good position,
surrounded from babyhood by comforts and kindness,
educated and favoured—to those of others. A keen
sense of the inequalities of life gripped his imagination,
and at the same time he was miserable because he was
utterly out of sympathy with the profession to which it
seemed he was predestined, and already yearning to
write, and to devote himself to the study of the art of
writing.   In this he was going against his father's
wishes, and the two, with the warmest affection for and
pride in one another, were continually brought into con-
flict in all their outlooks, big and small.

" My father would pass hours on the beach, brooding on the
waves, counting them, noting their least deflection, noting when
they broke. On Tweedside, or by Lyne and Manor, we have
spent together whole afternoons; to me, at the time, extremely
wearisome ; to him, as I am now sorry to think, extremely
mortifying. The river was to me a pretty and various spectacle ;
I could not see—I could not be made to see—it otherwise. To
my father it was a chequer-board of lively forces, which he
traced from pool to shallow with minute appreciation and
enduring interest. 'That bank was being undercut,' he might
say. 'Why? Suppose you were to put a groin out here, would
not the *filum fluminis* be cast abruptly off across the channel ?
and where would it impinge upon the other shore ? Or suppose
you were to blast that boulder, what would happen? Follow
it—use the eyes that God has given you : can you not see that a

great deal of land would be reclaimed upon this side ?' It was
to me like school in holidays ; but to him, until I had worn
him out with my invincible triviality, a delight." [1]

And, as in the aspect of the river, so in the aspect of
life. Their outlooks were entirely different. What interested Thomas Stevenson seemed to his son " extremely wearisome " ; what Louis Stevenson got out
of his opportunities seemed to his father " invincible
triviality." The tragedy was also the father's.

The height of it was reached with the realisation that
their difference in points of view inevitably showed itself
also in their religious outlooks. Louis Stevenson, of
course, suffered the usual youthful revolt from orthodoxy
in religion. Every high-spirited young man kicks against
any form of authority that stands in his way. Orthodox
creeds stand in the way. Many a young man has said in
his heart " there is no God," and fifty years later his last
state of intolerant orthodoxy is worse than his first state
of intolerant atheism. But poor Louis Stevenson had to
probe for his salvation through his father's very heart-
strings ; and, while his egoism spared his father nothing,
to his abnormally sensitive nature the process of making
his father miserable provided continual agony. But all
this was only the beginning, intermittent and fore-
shadowing, in the days when Stevenson swung down the
hill from Swanston into town, or hurried, cigarette in
mouth, up the windy North Bridge and into the gloomy
grey quadrangle of the old University. He was not
openly to break away yet.

Until 1871 it was supposed that Louis Stevenson was
to be an engineer, and his summer holidays still " took a
professional turn." In the summer of 1869, when he was
eighteen, he went with his father to Orkney and Shet-
land and the Fair Isle in the *Pharos,* the steamer of
the Northern Lights Commissioners—went the selfsame
voyage that fifty years before had given Walter Scott the
material for his *Pirate,* and had made him acquainted
with Stevenson's grandfather, " the official chief of the
expedition," when Scott had found him " a most gentle-

[1] *Family of Engineers.*

manlike and modest man, and well known for his scientific skill."

In the winter of 1869–70 Louis Stevenson took out the engineering class, and became " a favourite but irregular pupil " of Professor Jenkin's ; and that winter was a memorable one for him, for on February 16, 1869, he was elected to The Speculative Society, familiarly known in academic Edinburgh as " The Spec," of which he afterwards was to exclaim, " Oh, I do think the Spec is about the best thing in Edinburgh ! "

" It is a body of some antiquity, and has counted among its members Scott, Jeffrey, Horner, Benjamin Constant, Robert Emmet, and many a legal and local celebrity besides,"

he writes in *Memories and Portraits*. (The Minute Book is still kept open at the page where Scott, once secretary, spelt Tuesday Teusday.)

" By an accident, variously explained, it had its rooms in the big buildings of the University of Edinburgh : a hall, Turkey-carpeted, hung with pictures, looking, when lighted up with fire and candle, like some goodly dining-room, and passage-like library, walled with books in their wire cages ; and a corridor with a fireplace, benches, a table, many prints of famous members, and a mural tablet to the virtues of a former secretary. Here a member can warm himself and loaf and read ; here, in defiance of Senatus-consults, he can smoke." [1]

Alas, *tempora mutantur !* The Edinburgh student now smokes where he will, even in the faces of his passing professors.

But there is a greater privilege that the Speculative enjoys ; its right to its local habitation is not held under University regulations, and therefore its hours are independent. It can, like the House of Commons, indulge in an " All night sitting." Its Opposition can " obstruct."

And here, would-be orators learn and practise their craft, and clerics and lawyers and statesmen are made. If Waterloo was won on the playing fields of Eton, certainly the Reform Bill was passed on the Turkey carpet of the Spec.

In the March of his first year of membership Stevenson, like his hero in *Weir of Hermiston*, led a debate at the

[1] *Memories and Portraits.*

Spec in favour of the Abolition of Capital Punishment, and, also like his hero, found no seconder to his motion ; and the following week he read a paper before the Society on " The Influence of the Covenanting Persecution on the Scottish Mind " ; but—alas for the dignity of a member of the Speculative !—in that same winter Louis Stevenson was " run in " by the police during a " town and gown " snowball riot, and bound over by the City Magistrates to keep the peace.

In the spring and summer of 1870 Stevenson's holidays still leant towards engineering experience. He went expeditions with the University engineering class, and he spent a week at Dunoon looking after engineering work there, and three weeks in August on the little island of Earraid, off Mull, which was then being utilised as the headquarters for the building operations in connection with the deep-sea lighthouse of Dhu Heartach. Stevenson utilised it for other building purposes, for Earraid figures in *Kidnapped* as the scene of David Balfour's shipwreck. The trip to Earraid, via Oban, was greatly to Stevenson's taste, combining as it did open air and Scottish scenery with brilliant company. His former neglected teacher of Greek, Professor Blackie, was one of it, and Sam Bough the artist was on board the steamer —" with whom I am both surprised and delighted. He and I have read the same books, and discuss Chaucer, Shakespeare, Marlowe, Fletcher, Webster, and all the old authors. . . . I was very much surprised with him, and he with me. ' When the devil did you read all these books ? ' says he ; and in my heart I echo the question."

The open-air duties of his ordained profession were thoroughly congenial to young Stevenson. The office routine, a necessary part of his branch of the profession, he loathed ; but " hanging about harbour sides, which is the richest form of idling," was much to his loafing taste, and so were " wild islands " and " the genial dangers of the sea," and " the roaring skerry and the wet thwart of the tossing boat."

These things, he held, would go far to cure a youth " of any taste (if he ever had one) for the miserable life of cities." But alas, the miserable life of cities had already exacted its toll from young Stevenson. His parents, probably with anxious intentions for good, kept their young son on very short allowance of pocket money. He was treated as many a man treats a dependent wife, and as many parents treat dependent children;—he was allowed to share, and even command, what money can produce; but he was not allowed himself to handle money. The town house and the country cottage were both at his disposal; dinners his parents were ready to give for him and his friends; he might, had he wished, have run up accounts at his tailor's and his bootmaker's, and his parents would have paid them. But his sense of freedom and his individual tastes in spending had to be restricted to a pound a month for pocket money. The result was that Louis Stevenson became a Bohemian, the frequenter of what is called " low society," " scraping acquaintance with all classes of man and womankind."

"Looking back upon it, I am surprised at the courage with which I first ventured alone into the societies in which I moved; I was the companion of seamen, chimney-sweeps, and thieves; my circle was being continually changed by the action of the police magistrate. I see now the little sanded kitchen where Velvet Coat (for such was the name I went by) has spent days together, generally in silence and making sonnets in a penny version book; and rough as the material may appear, I do not believe these days were among the least happy I have spent. I was distinctly petted and respected; the women were most gentle and kind to me. . . . Such indeed was my celebrity, that when the proprietor and his mistress came to inspect the establishment, I was invited to tea with them; and it is still a grisly thought to me, that I have since seen that mistress, then gorgeous in velvet and gold chains, an old, toothless, ragged woman, with hardly voice enough to welcome me by my old name of Velvet Coat." [1]

" Petted and respected,"—a " celebrity." There is a touch in this that reminds one of the Miltonic Lucifer, with his " Better to reign in Hell than serve in Heaven."

It was at the end of the winter of 1870–71—a winter spent in non-attendance of the classes of Senior Mathematics, Natural Philosophy, Engineering, and Mechanical Drawing, in much private reading of both poetry and

[1] Quoted in Mr. Graham Balfour's *Life*.

prose, in attendance at the "Spec," (and in voting at that august assembly want of confidence in Gladstone's Ministry)—that Stevenson at last showed proof of having inherited a trait of his family's form of genius. At the end of March 1871, he read a paper to the Royal Scottish Academy of Arts on "A New Form of Intermittent Light for Lighthouses," which was adjudged "well worthy of the favourable consideration of the Society, and highly creditable to so young an author," and won him a £3 medal from the Society of Arts. How happy and proud must poor, much tried Thomas Stevenson, the father, have felt! How it must have seemed to him as if things might after all be shaping out rightly with his wayward son!

Less than a fortnight after, on 8th April, father and son took a walk to Cramond together—"a dreadful walk"—for, as they walked, Louis Stevenson told his father that he wanted to give up engineering, and to devote himself to literature as a profession. He must have made up his mind long before to tell his father this—all the weary months of winter—and the opportunity came that April day as they walked by the sea that they looked at so differently. No doubt the subject had come about by some talk of Louis's Intermittent Light paper.

It is easy to decide after the event. We know now who he was who thus wished to devote himself to literature as a profession. But what had the father to judge from in that April of 1871? Since his childhood, Louis Stevenson had always striven at authorship—witness his *History of Moses* dictated at the age of six; and since he was a mere lad of sixteen, when his father had published the *Pentland Rising* pamphlet, and bought up most of the copies, he had always been writing—writing—writing. But he had done it in secret, as practice in the art he loved, and had shown his literary attempts to no one, and had destroyed, as being not up to his own standard, much of what he wrote. So all he had to show in justification of his wish to dedicate himself to literature was his undeniable gift of writing brilliant, egotistic letters, and a pile of deprecated MS.—essays, notes of his ramblings and travels, a life of his hero Hackerston of

Rathillet, a poetical play, *Semiramis,* and some dramatic verse dialogues, " Voces Fidelium."

And how did Thomas Stevenson take the blow ? He " met the request with calm," and was " wonderfully resigned." He assented to Louis's giving up engineering ; but, the pursuit of literature not being a regular profession, he wished him to read for the Bar. The one thing did not clash with the other, the training for the Bar would all add to his mental stock-in-trade as an author—it was, indeed, a case of " continuity of policy." Was the father unsympathetic in his moment of bitter disappointment ?

Moreover, the profession of Advocate, esteemed in Edinburgh as on a high level of social respectability, may, with the addition of brains or influence, in due time be made lucrative ; but Thomas Stevenson, when he proposed this career to his son, must have known that his son, like all young advocates without private means, would have to be supported for an indefinite number of years after he was nominally in practice. Was the father hard to him ?

Louis Stevenson agreed to read for the Bar ; and life went on as before, and the summer—a summer that lingered in its coming, as Edinburgh summers will—passed at Swanston, with occasional holiday journeys to Cumberland and elsewhere, and enlivened by much jotting in note-books, and nice selection of word and phrase. It was during this summer that the article on Colinton Manse was shaped

The following winter, 1871-2, Stevenson was elected one of the five Presidents of the " Spec," and on 24th November spoke at it against Communism. To the law classes which he took out at the University—Civil Law and Public Law—he seems to have given more serious attention than he had bestowed on his Arts and engineering classes, for he came out third in the Public Law class.

This winter Stevenson and three other members of the " Spec " evolved the idea of starting an *Edinburgh University Magazine,* and Stevenson contributed six papers to it.

"It ran," Stevenson records in *Memories and Portraits*, "four months in undisturbed obscurity, and died without a gasp. The first number was edited by all four of us, with prodigious bustle; the second fell principally into the hands of Ferrier and me; the third I edited alone; and it has long been a solemn question who it was that edited the fourth."

Stevenson was anxious afterwards as to how to meet his financial share of the failure on his allowance of a pound a month; but he observed, " Thank God, I have a father."

On 4th March—before the end of the session—he went for a change of air to Dunblane, and was there over a month. Office work, which he hated, was his again on his return, for he began work on 9th May at the office of Skene, Edwards & Bilton, W.S.—the work being " copying "—" just enough mind work necessary to keep you from thinking of anything else." And the copying clerk, of course, did not come under the notice of the senior partner of the firm, William Forbes Skene, the author of *Celtic Scotland*—a fact much regretted by Skene in after years.

Only the first months of that summer were spent in dusty Edinburgh, for at the end of July Stevenson went abroad with his friend Sir Walter Simpson, the son of the discoverer of chloroform. Until 1870, the Simpson family had lived at 52 Queen Street, which looks down over gardens to Heriot Row, and theirs had been a house in which Louis Stevenson had been happy and intimate.[1]

Sir Walter and Stevenson went first to Brussels, whence a letter describes with enthusiasm the joys of "drinking iced drinks and smoking penny cigars under great old trees," the band, the " lamplit foliage and the dark sapphire night sky, with just one little star set overhead in the middle of the largest patch," and the dark walks and white statues and the summer lightning blinking overhead.

From Brussels they went on to Frankfort, where they spent all August, studied German, and went every night

---

[1] The daughter of the house, Miss Eve Blantyre Simpson, has since written more than one delightful book about R. L. S.

to the theatre or opera. In October he was back in
Heriot Row, back at the University—Commercial and
Political Economy and Scots Law—back at the " Spec,"
reading an essay before it on 12th November, on " Two
Questions on the Relations between Christ's teaching
and Modern Christianity "—and back to his struggle,
the misery of ill-health.

And with the beginning of another year another form
of wretchedness descended on him. He was now two-
and-twenty, and had " read precociously and omnivor-
ously " since he was a boy—first the Covenanting writers,
then English poetry—verse and fiction—the essayists,
French and English, French fiction, history, chiefly
Scottish ; and in turn he had had his favourite among the
authors—Dumas when he was thirteen, the Gospel of St.
Matthew, Balzac, Herbert Spencer, Walt Whitman. . . .

And he was now two-and-twenty, the product of precocious and omnivorous reading, the victim of an over-
eager restless conscience. During the last two years at
least he had begun to revolt from conformity in religion,
and to refuse to accept the Christian dogma in which he
had been brought up to believe.

On the last day of January 1873, father and son were
sitting together in Heriot Row—it must have been late,
for Louis had returned home from spending the evening
with his friend Charles Baxter, to whom the following
Sunday he wrote a wildly agonised letter about it all :

" In the course of conversation, my father put me one or two
questions as to belief, which I candidly answered. I really
hate all lying so much now—a new found honesty that has
somehow come out of my late illness—that I could not so much
as hesitate at the time ; but if I had foreseen the real hell of
everything since, I think I should have lied, as I have done
so often before. I so far thought of my father, but I had
forgotten my mother. And now ! they are both ill, both silent,
both as down in the mouth as if—I can find no simile. You
may fancy how happy it is for me. If it were not too late,
I think I could almost find it in my heart to retract, but it
is too late ; and again, am I to live my whole life as one
falsehood ? Of course, it is rougher than hell upon my father,
but can I help it ? They don't see either that my game is not

the light-hearted scoffer ; that I am not (as they call me) a careless infidel. I believe as much as they do, only generally in the
inverse ratio : I am, I think, as honest as they can be in what I
hold. I have not come hastily to my views. I reserve (as I
told them) many points until I acquire fuller information, and
I do not think I am thus justly to be called 'horrible atheist.'

" . . . O Lord, what a pleasant thing it is to have just *damned*
the happiness of (probably) the only two people who care a
damn about you in the world. What is my life to be at this
rate. . . . If all that I hold true and most desire to spread is
to be such death, and worse than death, in the eyes of my
father and mother, what the *devil* am I to do ? Here is a good
heavy cross with a vengeance, and all rough with rusty nails
that tear your fingers, only it is not I that have to carry it
alone ; I hold the light end, but the heavy burden falls on
these two. . . ." [1]

Of course, it is exaggerated and hysterical, but it is
written only two days after a scene that must have tor-
tured him ; and Stevenson was not physically strong
enough to endure such mental torture without wincing.
There is a real cry of agony in it, for the boy loved his
father, and understood him. And the pathos of it !—
" I have not come hastily to my views," he feels—and he
two-and-twenty ! And " they don't see either that my
game is not the light-hearted scoffer "—nor was it,
neither then nor after. In that he was right. What a
sorry welcome for the new-found honesty, the outcome of
his late illness—possibly the best thing he had yet ac-
quired from all his illnesses and his readings !

It seems now inconceivable that his parents should not
have recognised that this son of theirs would have to
build up his own faith, and that the bricks he built it with
would not be beliefs accepted from others, but those
gained by his own searchings and probings, readings and
discoveries. " To present to him the blunderbuss of
conformity, and bid him stand and deliver, were an
attempt at intellectual highway robbery." [2] He was
always searching and probing, his eager intellect was
always questioning and discovering—was it likely to

[1] *Letters of Robert Louis Stevenson* (edited by Sir Sidney Colvin).
[2] *The Faith of R. L. Stevenson*, by the Rev. John Kelman, D.D.

stop short at investigation of the very problems most dear
to the soul of the metaphysical Scot ?   But, whilst the
rigidness of Calvinistic doctrines was exactly what was
responsible for sending Louis rebounding to the opposite
extreme of unbelief, by one of Nature's ironies, the Calvinism in his own blood made him take himself in deadly
earnest, and made him wrack himself on the wheel of
conscience.

And yet—the other side of the picture, and the poor
parents ! The mother, not intellectually strong enough
to cope with the situation, conventionally anxious to
smooth things down, and to see the two she loved good
and happy.   The father, so simple, so upright, so strong,
his religious convictions as deeply rock-bedded and im-
movable as the foundations of his deep-sea lighthouses,
and all his ways and doings steered by their faithful light.

And this only son of his—what a series of anxieties his
life had been to the father !   How much he had taken
from his father, how little had he given to his father !
Thomas Stevenson had borne with equanimity the disappointment of barely two years before, when his son
flung away from the family profession ; he must have in-
tensely disapproved of his ways of life and his choice of
friends : but now this last shocked all that was funda-
mental in his notions and character.   His son was, in his
eyes, an atheist.

Perhaps some day it may be discovered that the whole
system is wrong which allows the child—daughter or son
—to develop into maturity of opinion and character, and
to remain economically dependent under the parents'
roof, compelled to live their life and think their thoughts.

Stevenson at two-and-twenty was not only absolutely
dependent on his father's generosity, but had no outlook
save the same dependence for years to come. He no
doubt felt himself, and was in the eyes of his companions,
and to his little world, a man, in all the approaching
dignity of wig and gown in professional hours, and with
all the present charm of brilliant wit and new thoughts
and gay bearing in his social hours ; and yet he had ever
the consciousness that, with liberty to lead a luxurious

life and have his bills paid for him and his friends enter-
tained, he had only a pound a month pocket-money to
call his very own. As long as the system prevails which
allows one grown-up person to be economically dependent on another, so long will stone or brick walls hide
tragedies, and within them will spirits be daily broken
on the domestic knife-cleaning machine, and talents rot
and be thrown aside with spent tea-leaves and empty
egg-shells ; and the most sacred relationships—that of
husband and wife, or of parent and child—be subjected
to ignoble conditions.

The following months must have been months of
wretchedness. Coldness at home from those he best
loved ; abroad, in the beautiful city he best loved,
and which was also probably at its coldest in spring,
" draughty parallelograms," and " downright meteoro-
logical purgatory " ; his regular occupation office work—
copying (Louis Stevenson " copying " !—" just enough
mind work to keep you from thinking of anything
else " !). Add to all this a morbid conscience continually
gnawing, unusually poor health, and unwise friends.

It was Stevenson himself who saw the affinity between
himself and poor Fergusson the poet,—" born in the
same city ; both sickly, both pestered, one nearly to
madness ; one to the madhouse, with a damnatory
creed."

Truly, at one time it might have seemed to him as if he
were to follow the fate of Fergusson. It was perhaps the
darkest hour—or seemed so to him then—and it was just
before the dawn. Louis Stevenson was to be saved.

At the end of July 1873, he went to stay at Cockfield
Rectory in Suffolk, with Mrs. Churchill Babington, one of
the cousins of the old Colinton Manse days, and her husband, the Reverend Churchill Babington, Disney Professor of Archæology at Cambridge. There he met Mrs.
Sitwell, now Lady Colvin ; and so interested was Mrs.
Sitwell in the young genius whom she at once recognised
that she wrote to Mr. (now Sir Sidney) Colvin (then a
Resident Fellow at Trinity College, Cambridge), who was
also due as a guest at the Rectory, and urged him to

come sooner, that he might meet the "fine young spirit" she had discovered : and Sidney Colvin came.

How much this double friendship meant to Stevenson ! How much he, and the literary world that appreciates him, owes to it !

Mrs. Sitwell's immediate influence on him and help in his life may be best told in Sir Sidney Colvin's own words :

> "He had thrown himself on her sympathies in that troubled hour of his youth, with entire dependence almost from the first, and clung to her devotedly for the next two years as to an inspirer, consoler, and guide. Under her influence he began for the first time to see his way in life, and to believe hopefully and manfully in his powers and future."

Of his own share Sir Sidney does not speak so explicitly, merely adding deprecatingly, "To encourage such hopes further, and to lend what hand one could towards their fulfilment, became quickly one of the first of cares and pleasures." But it is not difficult to see what that helping hand did for Louis Stevenson—the helping hand of a man only about five years his senior, who yet had already made himself a recognised position as a literary and art critic, had that very year been appointed Slade Professor of Fine Art at Cambridge, and in whom young Stevenson found not only one who could set him on his feet both as a man and as a writer, but a friend such as it is given to few men to make, and whose friendship never failed Stevenson through life. "I don't know how to thank you," Stevenson wrote to him, only about two months later, "and I am afraid I do not even feel grateful enough—you have let your kindness come on me so easily."

A month at the Rectory, and Stevenson went back to Edinburgh in the beginning of September, full of new hope and heart—"I would not have missed last month for eternity." His new friends had had the discernment and experience to see, what his father had not seen, that "if he could steer himself or be steered safely through the difficulties of youth, and if he could learn to write with half the charm and genius that shone from his presence

and conversation, there seemed room to hope for the
highest from him." So they sent him north buoyed up
in his literary aspirations, and full of schemes for work.
It had all been planned out in the warmth of the Suffolk
Rectory ; he was to read for the Bar, as his parents de-
sired, but he was also to " get ready for publication "
some essays—one on " Roads," one on Walt Whitman,
and one on John Knox. Plenty of change of atmospheric
conditions in the three subjects !

Stevenson wrote almost daily to Mrs. Sitwell after his
return home, egotistic letters, as always ; brilliant letters,
the continuance of all the talk at the Rectory ; hopeful
letters, about his essays he was working at ; intimate
letters, the outpouring of all his thoughts and doings ;
pathetic letters, for gradually they concentrated on the
misery of the home trouble, which he had found waiting
again for him. Before he had been home three weeks he
writes :

"I have just had another disagreeable night. It is difficult
indeed to steer steady among the breakers ; I am always touching
ground ; generally it is my own blame, for I cannot help getting
friendly with my father (whom I *do* love) and so speaking
foolishly with my mouth. I have yet to learn in ordinary
conversation that reserve and silence that I must try to unlearn
in the matter of the feelings." [1]

And having written this, he went down to supper, and
came up again to tell his friend :

"I can scarcely see to write just now ; so please excuse. We
have had an awful scene. All that my father had to say has
been put forth—not that it was anything new ; only it is the
devil to hear. I don't know what to do—the world goes hope-
lessly round about me ; there is no more possibility of doing,
living, being anything but a *beast*, and there's the end of it. . . .
I say, my dear friend, I am killing my father—he told me
to-night (by the way) that I alienated utterly my mother—and
this is the result of my attempts to start fair and fresh and to
do my best for all of them." [1]

And the saddest of all was written next day. He had
lain in bed in the morning, he tells her (probably after a
sleepless night) and heard his father go out for the papers ;

[1] *Letters.*

"and then I lay and wished—Oh, if he would *whistle* when he comes in again! But of course he did not. I have stopped that pipe."

The continual fretting and depression and excitement told steadily on his health. He was weighed, and found "the gross weight of my large person was eight stone six!" A month later, to Mrs. Sitwell: "I am not at all ill . . . with tonics, decent weather, and a little cheerfulness . . . I shall be all right again." Next day, 15th October, he wrote to Mr. Colvin: "Of course I knew as well as you that I was merely running before an illness; but I thought I should be in time to escape. However, I was knocked over on Monday night with a bad sore throat, fever, rheumatism, and a threatening of pleurisy, which last is, I think, gone. If I don't get away on Wednesday at latest, I lose my excuse for going at all, and I do wish to escape a little while."

The "excuse" was that the Lord Advocate had strongly advised him, in his father's hearing, to go to the English Bar; and so it had been quickly arranged that he should go up to London and present himself for admission at one of the Inns of Court. An unlooked for escape came; for when Stevenson arrived in London, towards the end of October, he was so ill that it had to be medical examination instead of legal examination; and Sir Andrew Clark, whom he saw, found him suffering from nervous exhaustion and threatening of pthisis, and ordered him straight off to sunshine and peace—to "the Riviera *alone*, without anxiety or worry."

He left at once. His mother came up to London and saw him off on 5th November. He travelled by slow stages to the South, and there, chiefly at Mentone, the winter of 1873–4 was spent; and there Sir Sidney Colvin went at Christmas to visit him; and it was in December, while Stevenson was at Mentone, that there appeared in print his first contribution to regular periodical literature—his essay on "Roads," inspired at the Suffolk Rectory, discussed in letters with Mrs. Sitwell, refused by the *Saturday Review*, and accepted, through Mr. Colvin's help, by P. G. Hamerton, the editor of the *Portfolio*.

CHAPTER III

"R. L. S."

It is remarkable to see how, from the time Stevenson was emancipated and free to follow his own bent, the truant from classes and the systematic idler turned into a hard worker. Even at the very first, at Mentone, in spite of constant weakness and ill-health and nervous symptoms, he yet managed to write.

At first he was too ill to do anything save sit in the sun and feel an old man ; and, believing that he was not going to recover, he became morbidly anxious to spend as little money on himself as possible, because, as he was dying, he would have no means of repaying the " huge loan which," by the hands of his father, " mankind had advanced." This idea took so firm a hold on his imagination that he grudged what he spent, and denied himself all but bare necessities. In these days, after he had been only a few weeks at Mentone, he wrote to Mrs. Sitwell :

"As an intellectual being I have not yet begun to re-exist ; my immortal soul is still very nearly extinct. . . Being sent to the South is not much good unless you take your soul with you, you see : and my soul is rarely with me here. I don't see much beauty. I have lost the key ; I can only be placid and inert, and see the bright days go past uselessly one after another. . . If you knew how old I felt ! I am sure this is what age brings with it—this carelessness, this disenchantment, this continual bodily weariness. I am a man of seventy : O Medea, kill me, or make me young again ! "[1]

So thoroughly was Stevenson the artist, that this very cry for his lost soul and lost sense of beauty and lost youth was presently to be used as " copy " for his article, " Ordered South."

A more hopeful frame of mind was brought about by a visit from Mr. Colvin, and by the cheerful and congenial coterie at the hotel to which Mr. Colvin, after they had had a few days together at Monte Carlo, took him. Especially delightful was the society of two Russian

[1] *Letters.*

ladies with fascinating children. " Children are certainly too good to be true," Stevenson declared.

Something perhaps was due also to a certain cloak, which Mr. Colvin, seeing that Stevenson had " no adequate overcoat " for the very cold weather, was commissioned to buy for him in Paris, and describes as suited to Stevenson's taste for the picturesque, and " piratical in appearance . . . in the style of 1830–40, dark blue and flowing, and fastening with a snake buckle." This cloak figures constantly in Stevenson's after letters :

"My cloak is the most admirable of all garments," he wrote to his father, "for warmth, unequalled ; for a sort of pensive, Roman stateliness, sometimes warming into romantic guitarism, it is simply without concurrent ; it starts alone. If you could see my cloak, it would impress you." [1]

And again, to his mother :

"It is a fine thought for absent parents that tneir son possesses simply the greatest vestment in Mentone. It is great in size and unspeakably great in design ; *qua* raiment, it has not its equal." [1]

The boy is as innocent a *poseur* as a peacock spreading its tail.

During the first month at Mentone, Stevenson made a brave attempt, in spite of bodily and mental weariness, to begin work on his *Walt Whitman ;* but he had to give up the attempt. Later, however, he wrote to Mrs. Sitwell that he had again tackled it, and it " at last looks really well " ; and on 5th February the essay " Ordered South " was finished, and Mr. Colvin sent it off to the then editor of *Macmillan's Magazine,* Sir George Grove, who accepted it.

At the beginning of April 1874 Stevenson left Mentone. He first went to Paris, where his cousin, R. A. M. Stevenson, was painting, and then, late the same month, returned home to Edinburgh. Absence had so far improved matters. Louis Stevenson took up his old life again under more favourable conditions. In the first

[1] *Letters.*

place, the strain of the relationship between father and son was relaxed, and they met with a new and happier understanding. In the second place, Stevenson's health was improved, and so was his mood of mind. Thirdly, Stevenson, owing to the help and encouragement of his new friends, Mrs. Sitwell and Mr. Colvin, returned to parents and to Edinburgh and to his reading for the Bar with the knowledge that he had already made a good start in the profession to which he intended to devote himself—that of letters. " Ordered South " was published in *Macmillan's Magazine* for May 1874, at the psychological moment of his return ; and during that same month John Morley asked him to write—and he wrote— a notice for the *Fortnightly* of Lord Lytton's *Fables in Song*. Also, his article on " Victor Hugo " was accepted for the *Cornhill* by Leslie Stephen, who wrote him a long letter of respectful criticism and encouragement. And the six months of independence had brought about another change. Stevenson was not asked to go back to the five shillings a week pocket-money of his student days, but was allowed seven pounds a month by his parents, and felt himself a man of means, and free, for that time at least, of money worries. " I have now an income of £84, or as I prefer to put it for dignity's sake, two thousand one hundred francs, a year." After his six months of independence abroad, he was never again to live continuously at home for more than a few months at a time.

May was spent at Swanston. In June, an acknowledged author, with articles printed by, or accepted by, three of the chief periodicals of the day, he went up to London and stayed with Mr. Colvin at Hampstead, was elected to the Saville Club, and met some of the literary people of London.

After his return, anxiety about his cousin, R. A. M. Stevenson, who had diphtheria severely, affected Stevenson's health, and he was ordered off for a yachting cruise on the West coast with Mr. T. Barclay and Sir Walter Simpson.

In August he went with his parents a holiday tour to
Chester, Barmouth, and Llandudno, and later in autumn
went a walking tour in Buckinghamshire. But all this
summer he was busy on and off with his pen—practising
himself in essays and stories and criticisms; shaping his
Walt Whitman paper and his articles on " John Knox
and his relations with Women " (which he privately called
"Knox and his Females"); attempting another paper for
the *Portfolio*, which had taken his first " Roads "; and
working at his tract, " An appeal to the Clergy of the
Church of Scotland."

" John Knox and his Females " was published that
autumn in *Macmillan's Magazine.* " An Appeal to the
Clergy of the Church of Scotland " was to appear as a
pamphlet next year, and apparently to make no appeal
whatever either to the Clergy of the Church of Scotland
or to anyone else.

Next winter (1874-5) brought Stevenson back to
Edinburgh again, to attend law classes at the University
—Scots Law, Conveyancing, and Constitutional Law and
History—again to work at the office of Skene, Edwards,
and Bilton ; again to hold aloof from the gatherings of his
social equals, to prefer the society of " all classes of men
and womenkind " ; to wander about in the country roads
and the Old Town slums in dirty, strange attire and with
long hair ; to be laughed at and very unpopular, and to
be much tried in health.

It was during this winter that, on 13th February, a
holiday and a Saturday, Leslie Stephen, who was in Edinburgh lecturing, took Stevenson to the Old Infirmary to
see " a poor fellow, a sort of poet who writes for him,"
as Stevenson described the pathetic creature who had
been in hospital a year and a half, and who " sat up in his
bed with his hair and beard all tangled, and talked as
cheerfully as if he had been in a king's palace." This
was Stevenson's first introduction to W. E. Henley, with
whom he soon formed a close friendship. " I shall try
to be of use to him," he told Mrs. Sitwell ; and he returned to the Infirmary armed with books—chiefly Balzac

—and he brought his friend Charles Baxter to see the invalid.

During this winter Louis Stevenson took part, for the last time, in Professor and Mrs. Jenkin's private theatricals—a historic function that for many years was one of the chief events of the Edinburgh winter. After long weeks of rehearsals, the actual performances began in April.

"Louis Stevenson was not one of the chief actors in that brilliant little company. Yet there are people who still remember his Orsino, in *Twelfth Night*—the slender figure in the 'splendid Francis I clothes, heavy with gold and stage jewellry,' and the satisfied languor of his opening words:

> 'If music be the food of love, play on,
> Give me excess of it, that, surfeiting,
> The appetite may sicken, and so die.
> That strain again! it had a dying fall.'

"But it was not so much the play that Louis Stevenson enjoyed, nor even the 'thrill of admiration' in successive audiences, as 'to sup afterwards, with those clothes on,' amid all the Shakespearian wit and raillery and badinage that circulated about that happy supper-table. 'That,' he wrote, 'is something to live for.'" [1]

In April, as soon as the University classes and Professor and Mrs. Jenkin's theatricals were both over, Stevenson left Edinburgh, and paid his first visit to Fontainebleau—afterwards so dear and familiar to him— with his cousin R. A. M. Stevenson, the artist. He stayed only a short time, and was back the same month in Edinburgh, at the Bridge of Allan with his father, entertaining Sir Walter Simpson and Charles Baxter for the "week end" at Swanston, and taking Henley, whose *Hospital Verses* had been brought out by Leslie Stephen in the *Cornhill*, for drives.

"I had a business to carry him down the long stair, and more of a business to get him up again, but while he was in the

---

[1] *Louis Stevenson: Some Impressionist Memories.* By Flora Masson, *Pall Mall Magazine*, November 1910.

carriage it was splendid. It is now just the top of spring with us. The whole country is mad with green. To see the cherry-blossom bitten out upon the black firs, and the black firs bitten out of the blue sky, was a sight to set before a king. You may imagine what it was to a man who has been eighteen months in an hospital ward. The look of his face was a wine to me."[1]

Stevenson's final examination for the Bar was to take place in July; but in June, instead of " grinding " for it, he wrote an article, inspired by his days at Fontainebleau —an article published afterwards as " Forest Notes " in *Cornhill*.

All this time he was constantly writing—constantly full of literary plans and projects. He was a thorough artist in temperament, and to him his work was the one thing real, and in homely phrase, " it took a good deal out of him."

" I find my stories affect me rather more perhaps than is wholesome. I have only been two hours at work to-day, and yet I have been crying and am shaking badly, as you can see in my handwriting, and my back is a bit bad."[1]

In the first joy of literary conceptions, he would write ecstatically and commend what he was composing ; but, soon after, much of what he wrote would be by himself condemned and destroyed ; and thus it is that much of work he tells about as on his anvil is now lost. He was, as well as being an indefatigable worker, a nice critic of his own work, his " reach " ever exceeding his " grasp " :

" Oh when shall I find the story of my dreams, that shall never halt nor wander nor step aside, but go ever before its face, and ever swifter and louder, until the pit receives it, roaring ?"[1]

On 14th July 1875, he passed with credit his final examination for the Bar, on 16th July was called, a week later received his first (complimentary) brief, and on the 25th sailed for London, *en route* for France. Here, with Sir Walter Simpson, he spent some weeks in the artist haunts round Fontainebleau, and studied French 15th Century poetry. Later, he joined his parents at Wies-

[1] *Letters.*

baden and Homburg; and when he returned to Edinburgh in autumn, it was with the virtuous intention of pleasing them by leading the life of a conventional young Edinburgh advocate. So he ordered a new dress-suit, and the old one was relegated to day use under the black gown, as was then the custom, and, "as gay and swell and gummy as can be," he frequented Parliament House, where they teased him by calling him Chatterton, and the "Marvellous Boy." "You know," he wrote to Mrs. Sitwell, "I lose all my forenoons at Court! So it is, but the time passes; it is a great pleasure to sit and hear cases argued or advised."

> "And at the Court, tae aft I saw
> Whaur Advocates by twa and twa
> Gang gesterin' end to end the ha'
> In weeg and goon,
> To crack o' what ye wull but Law
> The hale forenoon."

It amused him at first, but very soon grew irksome; and it was a great waste of his time.

During all this time he did journalistic work for the *Academy* and *Vanity Fair*—one contribution to the latter paper being a short review of Browning's *Inn Album*. "I have slated R. B. pretty handsomely," he boasted with glee.

By the end of 1875 he had very naturally managed to get through his income of "two thousand one hundred francs," and was reduced to six shillings in hand and was deep in debt; he attributed the debt chiefly to the new dress-suit. But though he refused all Mr. Colvin's invitations to London because of his impecunious state, he did manage during the winter to spend a month there, besides going a tour in Ayrshire and Galloway. To anyone who knows what would be the ordinary and legitimate expenses of a young man of his position in Edinburgh, it must be clear that poor Stevenson's allowance, from first to last, was, to say the least of it, mismanaged. Eighty-four pounds a year may have seemed wealth to

him after five shillings a week ; but eighty-four pounds
a year, if it had to cover his dress and his holidays, was
barely enough, and was not in keeping with his home-life.
Moreover, if it was paid to him in monthly instalments
of seven pounds at a time, the method was one that made
it almost impossible for him to keep out of debt.   For
seven pounds would never have been enough to meet any
big call, and yet leave him enough in hand.   It would
not, for example, pay for a holiday, nor for a new dress-
suit.   So he left his dress-suit owing at his tailor's.

It was during the following year, 1876, that Stevenson
began to contribute brilliant essays to the *Cornhill*, essays
later on to be published with the now familiar titles, *Virginibus Puerisque* and *Familiar Studies of Men and Books*.

In the late summer of 1876 he visited the Jenkin
family in the West Highlands, and afterwards went with
Sir Walter Simpson his canoe journey from Antwerp to
Grez.   This gave him the material for his first book, *An
Inland Voyage*, published eighteen months later.   The
tour ended at Grez, where the two young travellers found
the artist community somewhat diffidently and curiously
awaiting the arrival in their midst of a woman artist
seeking country quarters after study in Paris.   The
woman artist arrived, and proved to be an American,
Mrs. Osbourne, with a young daughter and a son.

The careless, Bohemian, artistic life of the forest
which had so great an attraction for Stevenson continued, and with it now was the greater attraction of
Mrs. Osbourne's presence.

Her life had not been happy in its domestic relations,
and this, which alone would have appealed to Stevenson's
chivalry, no doubt enhanced, in those idle congenial days,
the charm that drew him and fixed him, and settled his
fate on earth.

It was October before he returned to mundane life,
with everything outwardly unchanged.   For the next two
years his life ran on much the same tracks as before.   He
spent his time between Edinburgh, where he never
practised ;   London, where his headquarters were the

Savile Club; and Fontainebleau. It was at the Savile
Club, in January 1877, three months after his return
from the momentous time spent at Grez, that he met
Gosse, to whom he was introduced by Mr. Colvin, and
whom he " dazzled " by his brilliant talk, gaiety, and his
many-sided outlook on life. Part of February, and of
June and July, were spent in France, and after a brief
time at home, in Cornwall with his parents and in the
Scilly Isles with his mother, he returned to France in
August, and remained till November.

Though this year he did not seem to accomplish much
in the way of writing, for his literary output was chiefly
stray journalism, two or three essays in the *Cornhill*, and
work done for *The London*.[1] But in October the tale
" A Lodging for the Night," was printed in *Temple Bar*.
If to *Temple Bar* belongs the honour of printing Stevenson's first fiction, the *Cornhill* was not long in following
its example, and " Will o' the Mill " appeared in its pages
the following January (1878), and *Temple Bar* had also
that month another, " The Sire De Malétroit's Door."
From this time onward Stevenson's genius found expression more and more in fiction, instead of in the essays
that were its first vehicle.

During this year, 1878, the days that Stevenson spent
in Scotland might almost have been counted on the
fingers of his two hands. It was in April that, while
staying with his parents at Burford Bridge, he met and
made friends with George Meredith, " long honoured."
In May he saw his first book published—*An Inland
Voyage*, the publishers being Kegan, Paul, Trench & Co.
All that summer he spent in Paris, acting as private
secretary (the only regular post he ever filled in all his
life) to Professor Jenkin, who was juror at the Paris
International Exhibition; and in autumn he spent a
month at Monastier in Velay, and, having " finished

---

[1] A weekly review edited first by Glasgow Brown—an old friend
of " Spec " days, and one of Stevenson's joint editors of the ill-
fated *Edinburgh University Magazine*—and afterwards by W. E.
Henley.

Arabian Nights and Edinburgh book," and being " a free man," purchased a mouse-coloured donkey for sixty-five francs and a glass of brandy, and walked with this adorable companion through the mountains to Florac, and in winter wrote his *Travels with a Donkey in the Cevennes*.

On his return he stayed for a little at Cambridge, occupying Professor Colvin's rooms in his absence. But the classic atmosphere did not inspire his muse. " I cannot work—*cannot*," he wrote to his absent host.

"Even the *guitar* is still undone ; I can only write ditch-water. 'Tis ghastly. . . Do you think you could prepare the printers for a possible breakdown this week ? "

" The Guitar "—" Providence and the Guitar "—was built on the pathetic story of some strolling foreign actors, husband and wife, whom he had met at Grez. It was afterwards taken by *The London*, and Stevenson, always generous and warm-hearted, sent the money he received for it straight to the poor actors.

1878, his last year before he broke up his life, was what literary critics call " very productive," and the productions were of high literary order, and showed surprising range of subject. It was the year that saw, in May, the publication of his first book, *The Inland Voyage*, and the year in which he contributed the greater number of his series of essays to the *Cornhill*. He also had fiction in the *Cornhill ;* and " Providence and the Guitar," and the " New Arabian Nights " both came out in *The London ;* and *Picturesque Notes on Edinburgh* belongs to this year, for it was written in France in the summer, and published in the *Portfolio*, and went to press in book form at the end of the year. In the autumn and winter he wrote *Travels with a Donkey in the Cevennes*, and planned *Deacon Brodie* and other plays with Henley. In spring (1879) he wrote " On some aspects of Burns " for *Cornhill* —included later in *Familiar Studies of Men and Books*, and at Swanston drafted, and laid by, the four first chapters of *Lay Morals*.

In April he went to Shandon Hydropathic on the

Gareloch, *cum parentibus.* In May he went to London and stayed with George Meredith, and then spent till the end of June in France. His third book, *Travels with a Donkey in the Cevennes,* came out during the month, and in July he wrote to Professor Colvin:

"Meredith has been staying with Morley, has been cracking me up, he writes, to that literary Robespierre; and he (the L.R.) is about, it is believed, to write to me on a literary scheme. Is it Keats, hope you? My heart leaps at the thought." [1]

He was not yet twenty-nine, and he had been only six years, since the printing of his "Roads," a professional author. And what point had he reached in the career he had chosen? In spite of his frail health, in spite of being handicapped by never having a sufficient or independent income, he had so utterly overcome the persistent idleness of his student days, and become so industrious a worker, that he had in these six years, out of the literary *pabulum* he could command, achieved three books, about six-and-twenty critical and social essays, and five short stories in magazines and periodicals—mostly in *Cornhill* —and two long serials, afterwards to be reprinted in book form; besides much MS. either rejected by himself, or to be used later. And all this of a literary quality and finished grace of style which, while they did not appeal to "the general," caused literary judges to hail him as a "new artist of first promise in English letters."

. . . Mrs. Osbourne had returned to America the previous autumn with her daughter and son, to seek a divorce for herself from her husband. Stevenson, this summer of 1879, heard of her being seriously ill, and that she would be able to obtain the divorce.

He returned from abroad in the middle of July, and was in Edinburgh, at Heriot Row, for about a fortnight. On July 29th he wrote from there to Gosse:

"My enthusiasm has kind of dropped from me. I envy you, your wife, your home, your child—I was going to say your cat. There would be cats in my home too, if I could but get

---

[1] *Letters.*

it. I may seem to you the 'impersonation of life,' but my life is the impersonation of waiting, and that's a poor creature. God help us all, and the deil be kind to the hindmost ! " [1]

Next day he had made up his mind not to let his life be " the impersonation of waiting." He went to London, found all his friends there strongly disapproved of his project, knew his parents would do the same, and, without returning home to say good-bye or give any explanations, sailed on August 7th to New York. The circumstances of his going naturally made it impossible for him to ask for money from his father, and he had little of his own ; he therefore took his passage in an emigrant ship, the *Devonia.* It was done for necessary economy, but he consoled himself by the thought of literary copy, and he wanted also to test his power of supporting not only himself—as he had never done—but others, by his pen. He was so eager to prove this possible that he set to work at once, in all the discomforts on board, and wrote, during the ten days of the voyage, " The Story of a Lie," for the *New Quarterly :*

" Thirty-one pages in ten days at sea is not bad," he wrote to Mr. Colvin, as the *Devonia* neared New York. " If I fail in my great purpose, I shall see some wild in the West and visit both Florida and Labrador ere I return. But I don't yet know if I shall have the courage to stick to life without it. Man, I was sick, sick, sick of this last year." [1]

Arriving in New York on August 28th, he travelled in an emigrant train from Monday evening till the Saturday of the following week : " What it is to be ill in an emigrant train let those declare who know." At San Francisco he found Mrs. Osbourne better, and travelled on another 150 miles to the town of Monterey, and there—little wonder—broke down.

" I was pretty nearly slain ; my spirit lay down and kicked for three days ; I was up at an Angora goat-ranche in the Santa Lucia Mountains, nursed by an old frontiersman, a mighty hunter of bears, and I scarcely slept, or ate, or thought for four days. Two nights I lay out under a tree in a sort of stupor,

---

[1] *Letters.*

doing nothing but getting water for myself and horse, light
a fire and make coffee, and all night awake hearing the goat
bells ringing and the tree-frogs singing when each new noise
was enough to set me mad. Then the bear hunter came round,
pronounced me 'real sick,' and ordered me up to the ranche.
It was an odd, miserable piece of my life; and according to
all rule it should have been my death; but after a while my
spirit got up again in a divine frenzy, and has since kicked and
spurred my vile body forward with great emphasis and success." [1]

But Stevenson never recovered from that emigrant
voyage.

The next three months were spent at Monterey, an old
Californian town on the coast of the Pacific—" a lovely
place," Stevenson called it; and " The Pacific licks all
other oceans out of hand; there is no place but the
Pacific coast to hear eternal roaring surf." He lodged
with a French doctor, and had his meals at a restaurant
with a strange medley of other guests of all the nations
upon earth. He worked " as he had hardly worked
before "; and, above all, he pined for letters. His
letters to all the friends he had left are pathetic : his
irresistible gaiety and brave spirit show in them all, but
always comes the cry for home news. To Henley, in
October : " Do keep me posted, won't you ? Your
letter and Bob's made the fifth and sixth I have had
from Europe in three months." To Mr. Colvin, in
October : " I received your letter with delight ; it was
the first now that reached me from the old country " ;
and later : " I am now all alone in Monterey, a real in-
habitant with a box of my own at the P.O." To P. G.
Hamerton, in November : " A letter will be more than
welcome in this distant clime, where I have a box at the
post-office—generally, I regret to say, empty." Again
to Mr. Colvin in December : " I have never seen my
Burns ! " (in *Cornhill*) " the darling of my heart ! I
await your promised letter. Papers, magazines, articles
by friends, reviews of myself, all would be very welcome."

During the three months at Monterey he wrote the
essay on Thoreau, afterwards included in *Familiar*

[1] *Letters.*

Studies ; wrote his story, "The Pavillion on the Links," afterwards accepted, to his frank amazement—for he called it "blood and thunder"—by *Cornhill ;* he planned his *Prince Otto ;* he drafted, from the notes he had made during it, an account of his journey, to be called *The Amateur Emigrant ;* and he wrote a story, "A Vendetta in the West," which remained unpublished, as he was not satisfied with it. Eighty-three pages of this last, and about sixty pages of the draft of *The Amateur Emigrant*, were done before the end of the first month in Monterey, October. But it was money he wanted; he was writing in feverish anxiety to make money.

"It is dibbs that are wanted," he tells Henley. "Dibbs and speed are my mottoes. . . . At times I get terribly frightened about my work, which seems to advance too slowly. I hope soon to have a greater burden to support, and must make money a great deal quicker than I used."[1]

At the close of December he left the cheerful little coast town, where he had lodged with the doctor and played chess and discussed the universe with M. Simoneau, the restaurant proprietor, and went to San Francisco, where he lived in a workman's lodging of a single room, ate at cheap restaurants, and lived in "self-imposed penury " on 70 cents a day.

For a month he allowed himself a 50 cent dinner, and a 10 cent breakfast of coffee, rolls, and butter; ekeing out the butter that it and the roll might be finished simultaneously, for he could not afford a second pat. But at the end of January this amplitude was reduced to a 25 cent dinner ; and he wrote to Charles Baxter at home to sell his books and send him the proceeds.

In spite of all this his letters were still full of his almost boyish humour and his own unconquerable brave-hearted buoyancy of spirit ; yet at times the tragedy shows itself. The work he sends home is not so good, and his friends, as is right, jealous of his literary reputation, tell him so.

[1] *Letters.*

"You and Henley both seem to think my work rather bosh nowadays," he writes to Professor Colvin, "and I do want to make as much as I was making, that is, £200; if I can do that, I can swim; last year with my ill-health I touched only £109, that would not do, I could not fight it through on that; but on £200, as I say, I am good for the world, and can even in this quiet way save a little, and that I must do.

"The worst is my health. . . . But I don't know; I managed to write a good deal down in Monterey, when I was pretty sickly most of the time, and by God, I'll try, ague and all. I have to ask you frankly, when you write, to give me any good news you can, and chat a little, but *just in the meantime* give me no bad." [1]

And again:

"Everybody writes me sermons; it's good for me, but hardly the good necessary for a man who lives all alone on forty-five cents a day, and sometimes less, with quantities of hard work and many heavy thoughts. If one of you could write me a letter with a jest in it, a letter like what is written to real people in this world—I am still flesh and blood—I should enjoy it . . . man alive, I want gossip." [1]

And to Henley he writes:

"Do not damp me about my work; qu'elle soit bonne ou mauvaise, it has to be done. You know the wolf is at the door, and I have been seriously ill. . . . I have now £80 in the world and two houses to keep up for an indefinite period. . . . My spirits have risen *contra fortunam;* will fight this out, and conquer." [1]

But ill-health, overwork, penury, loneliness, and the great strain of anxiety overpowered the brave fighter. Two months after his coming to San Francisco he was lying at death's door—"pleurisy, malarial fever, and exhaustion of system."

A mere touch is all that is needed to send fluttering to earth a leaf that has been scorched by sun and nipped by frosts, and yet, frail and yellow, hangs persistently by its stalk. The touch, in Stevenson's case, was supplied by the illness of the little child of his landlord. Stevenson, so passionately devoted to little children, helped to nurse it.

[1] *Letters.*

For six weeks in March and April Louis Stevenson lay
dangerously ill, and was nursed back to life by the doctor
who attended him, and by Mrs. Osbourne.

"I have been very, very sick ; on the verge of a galloping
consumption . . . and I have cause to bless God, my wife
that is to be, and one Dr. Bamford . . . that I have come out
of all this, and got my feet once more upon a little hill-top,
with a fair prospect of life and some new desire of living. Yet
I did not wish to die, neither ; only I felt unable to go on
further with that rough horse-play of human life : a man must
be pretty well to take the business in good part." [1]

His illness, and the news that he was to be married,
brought about reconciliation with his parents, who,
never having been taken into his confidence, had judged
him from their own standpoint. When he heard of his
son's illness the father sent him twenty pounds—but it
never reached Louis Stevenson. In April "My dear
people telegraphed me in these words, ' Count on 250
pounds annually.' " And they sent money for their boy's
needs, and promised to receive and welcome his wife.

On May 19, 1880, Robert Louis Stevenson was married
to Fanny Van de Grift (Mrs. Osbourne), in the house of
the minister who married them, Dr. Scott, and with only
two other persons present, Mrs. Scott and Mrs. Williams,
the wife of Virgil Williams, an artist, and one of the very
few friends of Stevenson's San Francisco days.

After the marriage Louis Stevenson and his wife and
his stepson went straight to that Californian mining
town left in deserted ruins up in the mountains, now so
familiar from Stevenson's *Silverado Squatters*. June and
July were spent here, not without anxiety, for both Mrs.
Louis Stevenson and her son had diphtheria here.

On August 7, 1880, Stevenson, his wife and his stepson, sailed from New York for home. Was the day
chosen ?—or was it a coincidence ? It was exactly that
day one year before that young Stevenson, mad and
miserable, had started in an emigrant ship after his fate ;

[1] *Letters.*

and, cruel in his self-absorption, had left his parents without bidding them farewell or telling them where he was.
During the year he was to write of the father from whom
he had taken, as his due, so much, and to whom he had
rendered so little: " Since I have gone away, I have
found out, for the first time, how I love that man ; he is
dearer to me than all, except Fanny."

And now, after a year, when he again arrived at Liver-
pool, it was to find his father and mother, and Professor
Colvin with them, waiting there to meet and welcome
him.

Swanston, the " kintry hame," that Mr. Stevenson had
taken in Stevenson's boyhood, " to be so happy in "—
no doubt too full of memories, glad and bitter, of their
absent son—had been given up early that summer. So
Stevenson and his parents, his wife and her son, merely
passed through Edinburgh—Edinburgh was doubtless
deserted in August—and went straight up to the Highlands—Blair Atholl and Strathpeffer. Almost the first
thing that Thomas Stevenson did was to stop the publication, which both he and Louis were now adverse
from, of *The Amateur Emigrant*. The MS. was in publishers' hands, and Stevenson had received payment ;
but his father repaid them the sum, and the book was
withdrawn. It was here, at Strathpeffer, that Stevenson,
no doubt partly to please his father, evolved the plan
of another and very different book—a History of the
Union, and talked it over with Principal Tulloch, who was
at Strathpeffer. But all plans and talks were soon cut
short.

Parents and son and daughter-in-law had only about
two months together. Alas ! the year of ravage had
done its work too well. Stevenson's health had been
shattered. He now suffered from lung trouble, acute
chronic catarrh, and extreme weakness, and was told by
his uncle, Dr. George Balfour, that he must pass his
winters at Davos on the Alps. Sir Andrew Clark,
whom Stevenson again saw, confirmed this, and so to
Davos, late in October, Louis Stevenson and his wife,

with her son, and a little, very-devotedly-loved Skye
terrier of many names, all went.   But, in the two months
before they left, Mrs. Louis Stevenson had won her
father-in-law's heart, and, in Sir Sidney Colvin's own
words :

> " Parents and friends—if it is permissible to one of the latter
> to say as much—rejoiced to recognise in Stevenson's wife
> a character as strong, interesting, and romantic almost as his
> own ; an inseparable sharer of all his thoughts, and staunch
> companion of all his adventures ; the most open-hearted of
> friends to all who loved him ; the most shrewd and stimulating
> critic of his work ; and in sickness, despite her own precarious
> health, the most devoted and most efficient of nurses."

Truly, no longer did Stevenson try to run a race on
loose sand : his feet were set on firm rock.

What a debt Stevenson owed to women !   In his puny,
ailing infancy, his mother and his nurse Cummie had
soothed and tended him ; in his " troubled hour of youth "
he had found " an inspirer, consoler, and guide " in Mrs.
Sitwell, to teach him belief in himself ; in his moment
of failure, and struggle with poverty and death itself,
he had married a wife capable of being his comrade,
his critic, and his nurse.   With what confidence must
the father have seen his son again leave home, this time
in her care !   And yet, what must the parents have felt,
after their lonely year, as they gradually realised all the
year had meant to their son.   Who shall dare judge and
regret ?   For years Stevenson was to be an invalid,
with times of serious illness, and with constant pain and
weakness.   But there were two things that *made* Robert
Louis Stevenson—tried and tempered him as fire and
water try and temper steel—and the first of these things
was Work, and the second was Pain.

During the winter of 1880–81, spent at Davos, though
Stevenson found there only " a dream of health," and a
" dear hallucination," and fretted constantly at the cage
of hills that shut him in, and the wearisomeness of the
snows, yet there was much that he enjoyed in the life—
the skating and the tobogganning, the walks with that best

of comrades, his dog, and the toy printing-press that he
and his stepson played with like two boys together. He
was allowed to write for two, or three, hours a day, but,
though full of literary projects and dreams, he was too
ill to carry them out. Considering how weak he was,
and that he had no ready access to books, it was wonderful he achieved as much as he did. He wrote serial essays
—one on Samuel Pepys, for the *Cornhill*, one on " The
Morality of the Profession of Letters " for the *Fortnightly*, and four descriptive of Davos, which were
printed later in the *Pall Mall Gazette*—" Essays on
Travel." He also wrote several poems, long afterwards
to be included in *Underwoods*. Many of these were
in Scotch dialect. This was all he wrote, but he prepared for press his book of collected essays, *Virginibus
Puerisque*, and, having changed his plan of writing a
" History of the Union " to the even more ambitious one
of writing a " History of the Scottish Highlands from
1715," he began to read and to learn Gaelic, in preparation for this work, which was destined to be one of his
many discarded literary projects.

John Addington Symonds was living at Davos, and his
companionship was everything to Stevenson in his exile.
" It is such sport to have a literary man around . . .
eternal interest in the same topics, eternal cross-cause-
waying of special knowledge. That makes hours to fly."
But it was sadness too, for Symonds, also at Davos for
the sake of his health, by his presence, and his heroic en-
durance of his lot, kept his own fate constantly before
Stevenson's imagination. Stevenson, however, was com-
forted by the doctor's persistent assurance to him that
he would himself recover. Towards Christmas he was
buoyed up also by the anticipation of a visit from Mr.
Colvin ; but when the visit took place it was a time of
sadness. Mrs. Sitwell came unexpectedly to Davos, to
be with her son, and after months of anxious nursing she
lost him in April. His death inspired one of the poems
that are now to be read in *Underwoods*.

At the end of April, very little improved in health,

Stevenson returned with his wife—the young stepson
was now at school in England—and the dog, who was a
recognised member of the family, home to Edinburgh,
which he reached on May 30th, and where he spent three
days, and thence went with his parents to Kinnaird
Cottage, Pitlochry, and to Braemar.

It was in July, while he was at Pitlochry, that
Stevenson's restless nature showed itself in a singular
effort. He, hearing that Professor Æneas Mackay
was about to resign the Chair of Constitutional Law at
Edinburgh, actually offered himself as a candidate. He
tried for the Chair because, as he frankly explained to
the friends whom he asked for testimonials, the professor was required to lecture only for three months in
summer, and this would suit him well. Also, the emolu-
ments would make him " independent at once." How
he longed and chafed for independence ! He collected
thirteen testimonials, mostly from Englishmen who
knew not Scottish Universities, all of them from men
who loved Stevenson with a love that took no cognisance
of his knowledge of Constitutional Law. Among them
were Professor Colvin, Mr. Gosse, P. G. Hamerton,
Addington Symonds, Leslie Stephen, Andrew Lang,
and Mr. Charles (now Lord) Guthrie.

But letters asking for testimonials were not all he
wrote at Pitlochry. Here, in the air of his native country,
which singularly disagreed with him, and rapidly
undid whatever little good the winter at Davos had
accomplished, he yet got back to his fiction, composing
"Thrawn Janet" at Pitlochry, and "The Merry Men."
And at Braemar he began the two of all his books which
have perhaps brought him most fame and popularity—his
Child's Garland of Verses and his *Treasure Island*. The
public owes *Treasure Island*, it is said, to the literary advice of Stevenson's stepson, who had joined the family
for his holidays and who asked his stepfather if he could
write " something interesting." It owes much also to
Thomas Stevenson, who was deeply interested in the
book, and supplied much skilled knowledge of things

nautical to its construction. On August 2nd, after two months at Pitlochry, they went to Braemar, where they received visits from Professor Colvin, Charles Baxter, Dr. Japp, and Mr. Gosse.

Later in August he had bad hæmorrhage, and wrote : " I have so many things to make life sweet to me, it seems a pity I cannot have that other one thing—health."

And so, with the Edinburgh candidature pending, and nineteen chapters of *Treasure Island* written, they left Braemar on September 23rd, and returned to Davos *via* Edinburgh, London, and Paris, reached there on October 18th, and took up their quarters at a châlet near Addington Symonds's house.

This winter of 1881–82, the second winter spent at Davos, was a record year for bad health and good work. Stevenson was constantly suffering, and Mrs. Louis Stevenson was very seriously ill, and was obliged to leave him to go to Berne to consult doctors. Stevenson, helplessly left behind, missing her companionship and anxious about her health, wrote for solace to Charles Baxter :

"We have been in miserable case here ; my wife worse and worse ; and now sent away with Lloyd for sick nurse, I not being allowed to go down. I do not know what is to become of us ; and you may imagine how rotten I have been feeling, and feel now, alone with my weasel dog and my German maid, on the top of a hill here, heavy mist and thin snow all about me, and the devil to pay in general. I don't care so much for solitude as I used to ; results, I suppose, of marriage.

" Pray write me something cheery. A little Edinburgh gossip, in Heaven's name. Ah! what would I not give to steal this evening with you through the big, echoing college archway, and away south under the street lamps. . . . But the old time is dead also, never, never to revive. It was a sad time too, but so gay and so hopeful, and we had such sport with all our low spirits and all our distresses, that it looks like a kind of lamplit fairyland behind me. O for ten Edinburgh minutes—sixpence between us, and the ever-glorious Lothian Road, or dear mysterious Leith Walk ! But here, a sheer hulk, lies poor Tom Bowling ; here in this strange place, whose very strangeness would have been heaven to him then ; and aspires, yes, C. B., with tears, after the past. See what comes of being left alone." [1]

He went " down " and met his wife and stepson, and brought them back on Christmas Day; but Mrs. Louis Stevenson's illness continued a great anxiety. It was not till February that Stevenson reported: "My wife is better again. . . . But we take it by turns; it is the dog that is ill now."

And yet, the winter is one of achievement, for during it Stevenson finished *Treasure Island*, wrote most of *Silverado Squatters*, and the essays he contributed to magazines included "Talk and Talkers," and "A Gossip on Romance." By April he was able to report that since December he had done—

"90 Cornhill pages of magazine work, essays and stories: 40,000 words, and I am none the worse—I am the better. I begin to hope I may, if not outlive this wolverine upon my shoulders, at least carry him bravely like Symonds and Alexander Pope. I begin to take a pride in that hope." [1]

And so this winter, in the lonely snow-heights, and in Addington Symonds's company, strengthened Stevenson in other ways than physically.

The family returned to Scotland in May, breaking the journey north at Weybridge and at Burford Bridge, where Stevenson again met George Meredith. They arrived in Edinburgh on May 20th, stayed there till June, during which time Stevenson and his father went a week's trip together to Lochearnhead to collect fresh material about the Appin murder.

Stevenson seemed to be a good deal better in health; but the improvement was merely transitory—"a dream of health"; and the rude awakening came at Stobo Manse, near Peebles, where they went on June 26th. The place and the weather were both damp, and in a fortnight Louis Stevenson, whatever good had been gained at Davos all undone, went up hurriedly to London to consult Dr. Andrew Clark. On July 22nd, he went with

[1] *Letters.*

Professor Colvin to Kingussie, and there had brilliant
weather; but it was of no avail.

All this time, month after month, one after another of
his Davos articles appeared in *Cornhill*, and the initials
" R. L. S.," now so familiar to every lover of books,
began to be eagerly looked for, when each new *Cornhill* appeared, by the literary world of the day.

And, meanwhile, " R. L. S." was enduring great weakness after constant attacks of hæmorrhage. In early
September he left Kingussie and went again to London
to see Dr. Andrew Clark. It was decided that he should
not return to Davos, Mrs. Louis Stevenson having
suffered such illness there, and both she and Stevenson
himself being weary to death of the place. So it was
arranged that a home should be looked for in France, on
the shores of the Mediterranean, and in October (1882)
Louis Stevenson went with his artist cousin, R. A. M.
Stevenson, to choose it. The quest did not begin aus-
piciously. At Montpelier, Louis Stevenson had another
attack of hæmorrhage; his cousin had to leave, and he
returned alone to Marseilles, where his wife came to him.
Together, in three days, they found the house, " Campagne Defli," a sheltered one with a garden, near S.
Marcel, a suburb of Marseilles; and there they were
settled within a week, and had sent for their worldly
goods and chattels. But S. Marcel did not suit Stevenson. The attacks of hæmorrhage continued, and were
followed by fits of fever and exhaustion. He could not
work, and for a whole month was too weak to go beyond
the garden. Twice in one day he was insensible, and
" was for a long time like one dead."

In December a terrible epidemic of fever broke out,
and Mrs. Louis Stevenson insisted on her husband going
off immediately to Nice, while she—there not being
enough money in the house to permit of their both
making the journey—remained to pack up. For four days
no news came, and then the distracted wife went to Marseilles and telegraphed to stations and to the police,
and was gently informed by the police that her husband

had probably died and been buried—it often happened. More days passed—no news—and at last she received some, and went to Nice to find Stevenson reading the first letter he had received from her.

The two artistic temperaments calmed down after their anxiety, and went together to Hyères and stayed at an hotel, and, finding the place suited them, looked for a house there, and found what proved a perfect one—La Solitude, a châlet built after the Swiss fashion, and with a lovely garden and a wonderful view.

By the middle of February they got the Campagne Defli off their hands—" Mr. and Mrs. Robert Louis Stevenson were yesterday safely delivered of a Campagne," was how the invincible invalid announced it to Professor Colvin.

By the end of March, 1883, they were established at La Solitude, the same month Professor Colvin came to them—their first visitor.

" I was only happy once, that was at Hyères "—for here, where the climate suited him and the beauty of the view satisfied his soul, Stevenson's health improved so much that he hoped he was recovering, and here his writing was a joy and no fatigue. He wrote to Cummie to tell her of his Child's Verses, and that the book was to be dedicated to her. He was full of the book—choosing and rejecting name after name for it, trying to arrange illustrations for it; and then, in April, his head was " singing with Otto "—he had written four chapters in two weeks, and seven more next week. When, in May, he received £100 for *Treasure Island* he was in hilarious spirits, for he began to hope not only that he was recovering health, but that his ambition was at last to be fulfilled :

" It does look as if I should support myself without trouble in the future," he wrote to his father, from whom, barely two months previously, he had acknowledged £50 with careless brevity. " If I have only health, I can, I thank God. It is dreadful to be a great big man, and not to be able to buy bread." [1]

---

[1] *Letters.*

But it was yet to be two or three years before he was able by his pen to support himself and his wife and step-son, and during these years, as had been the case from the hour of his marriage, his father sent help whenever it was needed, " amply and ungrudgingly."

But neither Louis Stevenson nor his wife were good practical managers of money. If ever there were a case where a literary man should have been endowed by a grateful world with a liberal income, and set free to write, without having to trouble his dear head about money, that case was Stevenson, " willow-slender and as careless as the daisies." Every cheque seems to have been needed badly and used as soon as it came. " I don't like trying to support myself. I hate the strain and the anxiety ; and when unexpected expenses are foisted on me, I feel the world is playing with false dice." So he wrote to Henley, who was acting as his " unpaid Agent." And no doubt all that summer of 1883 " un-expected expenses " were " foisted " on him, for not only had the two flittings—to S. Marcel and then to Hyères—left him in debt, but his health must often have caused sudden expenses, and he had the education of his stepson to look after—and what were his earnings ? " This year, for the first time, I shall pass £300," he wrote, in September. Three hundred !

At that very time the *Child's Garden of Verses* was finished, " dedication and all " ; *Silverado Squatters* was in proof ; *Otto* " three parts done " ; and Stevenson was writing *The Black Arrow*, and eagerly expecting proofs of *Treasure Island*.

In May—the £100 for *Treasure Island* was probably not to be received till publication—he wrote to Professor Colvin :

"As usual, penniless—O but penniless : still, with four articles in hand (say £35) and the £100 for *Silverado* imminent, not hopeless. Why am I so penniless, ever, ever penniless ; ever, ever penny—penny—penniless and dry ?" [1]

In the autumn *Treasure Island* was published, and

[1] *Letters.*

E

brought him his "first breath of popular applause."
"To live reading such reviews and die eating ortolans—
sich is my aspiration."

In September, Stevenson heard of the death of one of
his early friends, James Walter Ferrier—he who had been
one of his fellow-members of the "Spec," and part-
editor with Stevenson of the *Edinburgh University Magazine,* and who had shared with Stevenson many of the
days of his "weather-beaten, Fergussonian youth."
Ferrier had been a young man of brilliant promise, and
his later life was a tragedy, and his death—coming after a
period of separation—made a deep impression on Stevenson's mind. "He is the first friend I have ever lost,"
he wrote to Miss Ferrier; and to his father, Thomas
Stevenson :

"Nothing that I have ever seen yet speaks directly or effica-
ciously to young men ; and I do hope I may find the art and
wisdom to fill up a gap. The great point, as I see it, is to ask as
little as possible, and meet, if it may be, every view or absence
of view ; and it should be, must be, easy. Honesty is the one
desideratum ; but think how hard a one to meet. I think all the
time of Ferrier and myself ; these are the pair I address. . . ." [1]

And, after this "great awakening," as Stevenson himself called it, there came into the happy, hopeful, hard-
working days at Hyères, a cold breath of anticipation,
to chill Stevenson's soul. His father's health showed
symptoms of failing, and he was subject to moods of
depression. The characters of father and son were anta-
gonistic even in this; and the son, who, well or ill, was
ever a delightful and cheering companion to those about
him—"The gay and vivacious Louis, whom, even in
the worst of health, I never once saw depressed" [2]—
writes with puzzled playfulness to the parents :

"I give my father up. I give him a parable: that the
Waverley novels are better reading for every day than the
tragic life" (Lockhart's *Life of Scott*). "And he takes it
backside foremost, and shakes his head, and is gloomier than
ever. Tell him that I give him up. I don't want no such a

---

[1] *Letters.*
[2] Lord Guthrie. Article in *Scotsman* on "Cummy."

parent. . . . What is man's chief end? Let him study that; and ask himself if to refuse to enjoy God's kindest gifts is in the spirit indicated. Up, Dullard! It is better service to enjoy a novel than to mump."

This letter was dated "last Sunday of '83." The next, dated "January 1st" (1884), tells the parents that the year closes leaving him with £50 in the bank, "owing no man nothing," £100 more due to him in a week or so, and £150 more in the course of the month; and that he can look back on a total receipt of £465, 0s. 6d. for the last twelve months, and

"When I think of how last year began, after four months of sickness and idleness, all my plans gone to water, myself starting alone, a kind of spectre, for Nice—should I not be grateful? Come, let us sing to the Lord!" [1]

And, within a matter of days, all his bright things had again come to confusion.

Charles Baxter and W. E. Henley paid him a week's visit to Hyères, and at its conclusion, early in January, he accompanied them to Nice, and was there felled by an attack of severe congestion of the lungs, complicated later by acute internal congestion. Here he lay at death's door, and at one time was given up. But he struggled back to life, and was taken home, partly recovered, to Hyères. Was his spirit beaten out of him? Not at all; by March he was writing mad, brilliant, cheery letters to his friends, and signing himself "The loquacious man at peace"; and signing it upside-down, to indicate he was writing from the horizontal. Two chapters of *Otto* remain, he told Professor Colvin, one to re-write and one to create, but he was not yet able to tackle them, and his restless, prolific mind was teeming with literary criticisms—"The Incredible Barbey d'Auré-villy, Lockhart's Scott, the Waverleys, the Bible—(the Bible, in most parts, is a cheerful book; it is our little piping theologies, tracts, and sermons that are dull and dowie)"—St. Augustine, the Shorter Catechism, and Charles Lamb—all in one brilliant letter.

[1] *Letters.*

But Fate had not done with him. To think of it is like seeing some horse, with wide eyes and straining muscles, patiently and bravely trying its best to pull too heavy a load up a steep hill, and being cruelly beaten and tugged by its driver.

In April he was again attacked by hemorrhage and sciatica, and he suffered with his eyes.

"I am too blind to read, hence no reading; I am too weak to walk, hence no walking; I am not allowed to speak, hence no talking; but the great simplification has yet to be named; for, if this goes on, I shall soon have nothing to eat—and hence, O Hallelujah! hence no eating."[1]

During this miserable time they had the comfort of Miss Ferrier's presence, for she had come to stay with them to Hyères in April.

In May he was again dangerously ill—hemorrhage of the lungs—and for weeks lay at the point of death; but again he struggled back to life.

"This has been a fine, well-conducted illness," he writes to Gosse, when he is recovering. "A month in bed; a month of silence; a fortnight of not stirring my right hand; a month of not moving without being lifted. Come! *Ça y est:* devilish like being dead."[1]

At the end of June he was taken by slow stages, first to Royat for a few weeks, and then to England, where a week or two were spent at Richmond. The doctors' verdict was favourable—they all held out hopes of ultimate recovery; but it was impossible to think of a return to Hyères, both on account of his health, and also because cholera had broken out there; and so, in September (1884), the family went to Bournemouth; and here, as it proved, amid the heaths and pines that are so like Scotland, Louis Stevenson and his wife were to make their home for nearly three years—till August 1887.

The first eight months were spent first in lodgings on the West Cliff; and then as tenants of a house named Bonallie Towers. One suspects Stevenson of having been biassed in its favour because of Bonaly Tower at

[1] *Letters.*

Colinton, once Lord Cockburn's home, and in Stevenson's day belonging to Professor Hodgson. At Easter the Stevensons moved to a house which Mr. Stevenson had in February presented as a gift to his daughter-in-law; a brick ivy-clad house, with a view of the sea from its upper windows, and a garden and a brook. In spite of the Married Women's Property Act, then in robust and healthy infancy, " I shall call my house Skerryvore when I get it," Louis Stevenson writes.

During these three years at Bournemouth Stevenson lived the life of a chronic invalid, chiefly in the sick-room, and suffering constant pain and weakness; and yet these three years proved a most industrious and successful time of Stevenson's literary life. Stevenson's brave spirit never yielded. To his father, whose failing health had produced characteristic fits of depression, he wrote in half humorous reproof:

"Fanny is very very much out of sorts, principally through perpetual misery with me. I fear I have been a little in the dumps, which, *as you know*, sir, is a very great sin. I must try to be more cheerful; but my cough is so severe that I have sometimes most exhausting nights and very peevish wakenings. However, this shall be remedied. . . . There is, my dear Mr. Stevenson (so I moralize blandly as we sit together on the devil's garden-wall), no more abominable sin than this gloom, this plaguey peevishness; why (say I), what matters it if we be a little uncomfortable—that is no reason for mangling our unhappy wives."[1]

To his friend Charles Baxter he is more explicit, but humorous still:

"We are all vilely unwell. I put in the dark watches imitating a donkey with some success, but little pleasure; and in the afternoon I indulge in a smart fever, accompanied by aches and shivers. I at least am a *regular* invalid. I would scorn to bray in the afternoon; I would indignantly refuse the proposal to fever in the night."[1]

To Miss Ferrier he wrote about the same time:

"But we'll no gie owre jist yet a bittie. We've seen waur; and dod, mem, it's my belief that we'll see better."

---

[1] *Letters.*

And yet, in these same early months at Bournemouth, he was deep in his "Arabs" (*More New Arabian Nights*); he managed to finish *Prince Otto* and the *Child's Garden of Verses*, both nearly completed at Hyères, and both published next year, 1885 ; he wrote his plays, *Admiral Guinea* and *Beau Austin*, in conjunction with Henley ; and he began a Highway novel, *The Great North Road*, which was never completed.

He still suffered a continual strain about money, thankfully accepting commissions for work that would bring immediate payment ; and constantly applying for help from home. "About money," he writes in December to his parents, who had evidently inquired, "I am afloat and no more," and he warns them that he will have to fall back on them at the New Year, "like a hundredweight of bricks," for doctor, rent, and chemist are all threatening. But all this must have been put right for him by the parents, for they came to Bournemouth and spent the winter with their son and daughter-in-law, and did not leave till after the gift of " Skerry-vore."

In November, Stevenson had accepted an order from Gosse for a Christmas ghost story for the *Pall Mall Magazine*, for which he was to receive £40 ; but when he could not on account of his health overtake the work, he sent the *Pall Mall* " The Body Snatcher " instead—a piece of melodramatic work written at Kinnaird at Pitlochry in 1881—and refused to take the full £40 for it. Henley seems to have remonstrated with him for this, and received a wholesomely indignant lecture from Stevenson in return :

". . . What are we ? Are we artists or city men ? Why do we sneer at stockbrokers ? O nary; I will not take the £40. I took that as a fair price for my best work ; I was not able to produce my best ; and I will be damned if I steal with my eyes open." [1]

In December, "I never sleep," he wrote; but he managed from five to seven hours' work a day, and on

[1] *Letters.*

January 4 (1885), he wrote in great joy to Professor Colvin to tell him he had been commissioned to write a volume on the Duke of Wellington for Longmans' *English Worthies*, and asked Professor Colvin for many books he needed for it. This life of Wellington was doomed to be one of many literary projects for which Stevenson prepared the material, but never accomplished. Stevenson had, in January, been on the eve of writing to Gladstone about this Wellington book, and had become aware " of an overwhelming respect for the old gentleman . . . by mere continuance of years, he must impose." But Stevenson was ever a Conservative, with firmly implanted Conservative principles, ever since the days when at the " Spec " he had voted want of confidence in Gladstone's government ; and moreover, in his heart he was a soldier, though fate had ordained he was only to conduct campaigns in play. In February came the news of the abandonment of General Gordon and his heroic death ; and among the thousands who were bowed by shame, no one felt it more bitterly than the invalid Robert Louis Stevenson, whose dream had always been, " Oh that I had been a soldier ! "

"I do not love to think of my countrymen these days; nor to remember myself. Why was I silent? I feel I have no right to blame anyone ; but I won't write to the G. O. M. I do really not see my way to any form of signature, unless 'your fellow criminal in the eyes of God.' "

And again :

"We believe in nothing, Symonds; you don't, and I don't ; and these are two reasons out of a handful of millions why England stands before the world dripping with blood and daubed with dishonour." [1]

In March of this year the *Child's Garden of Verses* was published, and a review of it by Mr. Archer led to a friendship between Stevenson and him. In June Stevenson lost one of his kindest friends in his former professor, Professor Fleeming Jenkin of Edinburgh. In the last months of this year Stevenson wrote what

[1] *Letters.*

proved to be an enormous popular success—*The Strange Case of Dr. Jekyll and Mr. Hyde*. It was published in January 1886, and " caught the attention of all classes of readers, was quoted from a hundred pulpits, and made the writer's name familiar to multitudes both in England and America whom it had never reached before."[1]

Four thousand copies sold in the first six months.

He was still writing *Kidnapped*, which he finished in March ; and from then to the end of the year he was busy preparing the materials for a life of Professor Jenkin. *Kidnapped*, after running for two months in *Little Folks*, was published in July, and proved at once another popular success. In autumn Stevenson paid a visit to Professor Colvin in London, at the British Museum, and there met many of the interesting people, literary and artistic, in London at that time ; among them Robert Browning.

From London, his health having stood his visit there, he ventured to Paris with Henley—again without a breakdown—and then returned to Bournemouth for another winter of ill-health. Part of this winter the parents again came to Bournemouth to be near their son, and spent some of their time at a house they rented there, and some at Torquay. On April the 1st they came back to Bournemouth from Torquay, but as the father's health grew much worse, on April the 21st they travelled home to Edinburgh.

During this very week that was to be his last week on earth with his father, a curious Quixotic project took possession of Robert Louis Stevenson's restless, conscience-ridden imagination.

He felt strongly on the subject of the lawless oppression exercised by the Fenians in Ireland, and his indignation was especially aroused by their persecution of the widow and daughters of a farmer who had been murdered by the Moonlighters. Stevenson conceived the idea of going to live on the farm, in County Kerry, and

[1] Sir Sidney Colvin. *Letters of Robert Louis Stevenson*, vol. ii., page 195.

would have done so, and Mrs. Louis Stevenson was prepared to go with him, under protest ; but the scheme had to be given up, chiefly on account of his father's health.

On May 6, a fortnight after his parents had left for home, Robert Louis Stevenson went for the last time to Edinburgh. He went in haste ; but he was too late for recognition. Thomas Stevenson died at 17 Heriot Row, on May 8, 1887.

His father's death, and his dying without recognising him, was a great shock to the son. He was ill, was not allowed to attend the funeral—" it was the largest private funeral in man's memory here "—and he never left the house, the familiar house of his youthful discontents and joys, till the end of May, when he returned to his sick-room at Bournemouth. There, for two months, he suffered much, both from illness and from " black depression."

On August 21, 1887, Robert Louis Stevenson, this time accompanied by his wife, his stepson, his widowed mother, and a faithful woman servant, Valentine Roch, who had been in their service for some time, sailed once again from London for New York.

The previous day, spent at a London hotel, he had seen and said good-bye to a large number of friends. On the day itself, it was the friend of all his friends, Professor Colvin, who went to the docks and saw him off. And of that parting Sir Sidney Colvin records : " Leaving the ship's side as she weighed anchor, and waving farewell to the party from the boat which landed me, I little knew what was the truth, that I was looking on the face of my friend for the last time."

CHAPTER IV

" TUSITALA "

AMERICA, so often the first to recognise our literary geniuses, was the first to accord Robert Louis Stevenson the dues of celebrity. *Treasure Island*, which had been out for five years, *Kidnapped*, and *The Strange Case of Dr. Jekyll and Mr. Hyde*, both of which had been out for over a year, had all attained immense popularity in the United States; the first two for their intrinsic merit as novels of adventure, and the third because of the even greater, if different, interest it had aroused.

So it happened that Stevenson, when, for the second time in his life, he landed at New York—instead of, as eight years previously, boarding an emigrant train, solitary and wretched, to arrive at his journey's end a physical wreck, and be nursed back to life in an Angora goat-ranch by a kindly old bear hunter—was this time surrounded at once by a crew of importunate interviewers, and rescued from them by eagerly hospitable friends. But Stevenson's health was the factor that had not improved. He caught cold on the Banks; and when, after one day at New York, he was carried off by his friends Mr. and Mrs. Charles Fairchild to Newport, it was " to go to bed and to grow worse, and to stay in bed until I left again."

After ten days of luxury and kind nursing at Newport, he returned convalescent to New York. Mrs. Louis Stevenson and her son meanwhile, it having been decided that the journey to Colorado was too long and the winter climate of Colorado too severe, sought and found a home for the family at Saranac Lake, in the Adirondack Mountains; and thither they all migrated towards the end of September, to live there for over six months.

Before they left New York, Stevenson had met old friends and made many interesting and congenial new friends, among them Mr. St. Gaudens the sculptor, to whom he had sat for his medallion, and Mr. C. Scribner, the proprietor of *Scribner's Magazine*. And he had received several orders for work, and wrote to Professor Colvin from New York, just before he left for Saranac :

> " I am now on a salary of £500 a year for twelve articles in Scribner's Magazine on what I like; it is more than £500, but I cannot calculate more precisely. You have no idea how much is made of me here ; I was offered £2000 for a weekly article—eh heh ! how is that ? but I refused that lucrative job." [1]

The house at Saranac, " a wooden house on a hill-top," known as " Baker's," pleased Stevenson because the surroundings bore likeness to Scotland. " The whole scene is very Highland," he says.

And again :

> " The country is a kind of insane mixture of Scotland and a touch of Switzerland and a dash of America, and a thought of the British channel in the skies . . . a decent house . . . on a hill-top with a look down a Scottish river in front, and on one hand a Perthshire hill . . ." [1]

But the climate exaggerated that of Scotland. The Stevensons had two thermometers, one called after its giver, " Gosse," hung inside the sitting-room, and was well accustomed to freezing point and below ; but the other hung in the veranda, and was there " condemned to register minus 40°, and that class of temperatures." *This* thermometer was called " The Quarterly Reviewer."

The bitter cold did not suit Mrs. Louis Stevenson, who had to go to New York for a month or so for her health ; and, the stepson being also away, Louis Stevenson and his mother kept house together for some time at the Christmas season on this bleak American hill-top. It must have seemed like the old days to mother and son. And the climate, in spite of its severity, suited Stevenson.

"I am wonderfully better," he wrote to Mr. Colvin in March 1888 ; "this harsh, grey, glum, doleful climate has done me

[1] *Letters.*

good. You cannot fancy how sad a climate it is. When the thermometer stays all day below 10° it is really cold ; and when the wind blows, Oh commend me to the result." [1]

There, in this " doleful climate," Stevenson managed during six months to do a great deal of writing, and solaced his leisure hours by playing on a flute. *The Wrong Box* owed its first beginnings to young Lloyd Osbourne, who tapped it out cheerfully in draft on his typewriter, to his stepfather's amusement. It was at Christmas time that Stevenson planned *The Master of Ballantrae*, and fell head over ears into the drafting of it : " No thought have I now apart from it," he confided to Mr. Colvin in a letter dated Christmas Eve. It was written red hot off the anvil, for by March the proofs of the first part began to arrive.

Soon all his thoughts were apart from his work ; for it was in this March month at Saranac that Stevenson received a letter from Henley at which he took umbrage, and which was the sole cause and beginning of the quarrel between them. Possibly, had the men been together, this quarrel, like others—for there certainly must have been many irritable passages and disagreements previously to this time—this quarrel would have blown over. But Stevenson was in no mood to see things in proportion. He was highly wrought; he felt wounded and hurt, and his wrath " worked like madness in his brain." And Stevenson was incontinent of letter-writing ; and if an angry man lets his anger find outlet in letter-writing, his wrongs inflame his imagination in the act. To throw a *casus belli* among sensitive, morbid, excitable temperaments, is like throwing a lighted match among shavings. They flare up. So these last days in America were embittered.

The original cause of the quarrel itself—the unfortunate quarrel which has caused so much conjecture and discussion and misapprehension—leaves no stain and reflects no dishonour on the character of either Henley or Stevenson.

In the middle of April (1888), the whole party left

[1] *Letters.*

Saranac and returned to New York, spending a fortnight there, and going thence to Manasquan on the New Jersey coast, where they stayed at a " delightful country inn " within sound of the sea. Mr. W. H. Low and Mr. St. Gaudens the sculptor came to see Stevenson here, and Stevenson spent happy open-air hours sailing a " cat-boat." Mrs. Louis Stevenson meanwhile went to San Francisco to see her relations, and while there made inquiries about a yacht suitable to charter for a cruise in the Pacific, and wrote and told her husband about the yacht *Casco*. Stevenson telegraphed his approval.

"I have found a yacht," he wrote to Charles Baxter, "and we are going full pitch for seven months. If I cannot get my health back (more or less), 'tis madness ; but, of course, there is hope. . . . If this business fails to set me up, well, £2000 is gone, and I know I can't get better. We sail from San Francisco, June 15th, for the South Seas in the yacht *Casco*." [1]

The £2000 of which he speaks was Stevenson money which he had inherited at the death of his father.

Three weeks of excitement and hope and preparation followed :

"It seems indeed too good to be true ; and that we have not deserved so much good fortune. From Skerryvore to the Galapagos is a far cry ! And from poking in a sick-room all winter to the deck of one's own ship, is indeed a heavenly change." [1]

On June 28, 1888, Robert Louis Stevenson sailed from San Francisco on the yacht *Casco*, with his wonderfully brave mother, his wife, and his stepson, and the maid-servant Valentine Roch, who had come to America with them from England.

And so he sailed, through the Golden Gate. . . .

Stevenson must have had lurking at the back of his mind, ever since he was four-and-twenty, a romantic glamour with regard to the South Sea Islands. It began one evening in Edinburgh in the June of the year 1875, when there dined at his father's house in Heriot

[1] *Letters.*

Row " an awfully nice man," the Hon J. Seed, formerly
Secretary to the Customs and Marine Department of
New Zealand. Late that evening Stevenson added to a
letter he had written earlier in the day to Mrs. Sitwell
a hurried postscript with his first enthusiastic reflection
of Mr. Seed's talk :

"Telling us all about the South Sea Islands till I was sick
with desire to go there : beautiful places, green for ever;
perfect climate ; perfect shapes of men and women, with red
flowers in their hair ; and nothing to do but to study oratory
and etiquette, sit in the sun, and pick up the fruits as they
fall. Navigator's Island is the place ; absolute balm for the
weary " . . .[1]

And so, that evening, the idea was planted in the
fertile soil of Louis Stevenson's imagination. It lay
dormant, but that the idea had not died is shown by the
allusion in *The Hair Trunk*, written in 1877.

It was four years later that the dormant seedling was
watered, for it was during the miserable time at San
Francisco that his friend Charles W. Stoddart lent him
Herman Melville's books, *Typee* and *Omoo*, and his own
book, *South Sea Idylls*,[2] and so revived the impression
made that summer evening in Edinburgh by the
entrancing talk of the " awfully nice man." No doubt
to the half-starved Stevenson of those San Francisco days—sick and sorry both in mind and body,
exiled, penniless, lonely, cast off and wretched—the
vision came again and made an intensified and irradi-
cable impression ; and in the streets of San Francisco he
was " sick with desire."

It was thus no new dream he fulfilled when, in his
thirty-seventh year, finding himself at last a man of
means, he spent his capital on the purchase of a yacht,
" and now in 1890, I (or what is left of me) go at last to
the Navigator Islands." Across the Pacific Ocean they
sailed, followed, till they reached the limit of the north-
east trades, by graceful pilot birds circling round them

[1] *Letters.*

[2] Published at home by Murray as *Summer Cruising in the South
Seas.*

and dropping down into the hollows of the waves; cutting
through the empty expanse of ocean, deserted by even
these fellow-voyagers, but by night hearing the eerie cry
of the " boatswains," who had succeeded them, flying
invisible between them and the stars overhead; seeing
the Southern Cross hang " thwart in the forerigging,"
and the pole star and the " familiar plough " drop low
and ever lower till it vanished.

The *Casco* sailed for the Marquesas, and on July 28th,
the day month from the day they had sailed, she dropped
anchor in Anaho Bay in Nukahiva—the very island of
Herman Melville's *Typee*, read long years ago at San
Francisco. Here the Stevenson party stayed six weeks,
and the first thing Stevenson did was to write to Sir
Sidney Colvin. They then cruised among the coral
islands in the Low Archipelago,—dangerous voyaging,
but " the interest, indeed, has been *incredible*. I did
not dream that there were such places or such races."

In October they made the Tahitian group, or " Society
Islands," and at the chief town, Papeete, Stevenson fell
ill, and went to the other and milder side of the island
to recruit. Here, at Tautira, which Stevenson called
" the garden of the world," " mere Heaven," and " first
chop," he made friends with Ori a Ori, a local chief, whom
he described as " exactly like a Colonel in the Guards,"
—" six feet three in his stockings, and a magnificent
man," and " one of the finest creatures extant." Stevenson and this chief exchanged names—a great mark of
friendship,—and Stevenson lived in Ori a Ori's house for
two months, while the masts of the *Casco* were under
repair. And at Tautira,—strange incongruity of subject !—Stevenson made great advance with *The Master
of Ballantrae.*

So ended the year 1888 ; and on Christmas Day, the
masts being repaired, the Stevensons sailed for Honolulu,
and Ori a Ori ran along the beach to see Louis Stevenson
still, and cried out " Farewell, Louis," and watched the
vanishing ship till the night fell.

Stevenson went to Honolulu to gather his mails, and

from them to discover his financial position, and from it
to determine the route by which he should travel home.
By whatever route he reached Southampton he would,
he wrote to Sir Sidney Colvin, " like fine to see you on
the tug." But it all depended, he thought, on whether
he had any money awaiting him at Honolulu, and with
regard to this he anticipated " the devil of an awakening "
from " a mighty pleasant dream." A pleasant dream it
had been—a dream of renewed health, of a life of open
air adventure and peril, of keen interest in totally new
surroundings, and of new races and new friendships.
All this tempted him to stay; but two things, he told
Charles Baxter, drew him home,—his stepson's prospects,
and the thought of " Colvin, to whom I feel I owe a sort
of filial duty." And yet—the Pacific and its fairyland,
its climate and health, lay before him; and if he returned to England it would be " to go to bed again."

The yacht *Casco* was paid off at Honolulu, and they
stayed there six months. By March their plans were
made. Mrs. Stevenson was to return home to Scotland
early in May; but for Louis Stevenson and his wife and
stepson the Pacific voyages were to be begun again in
June for another year, and the home-coming was to be
postponed to the summer of 1890. It was a letter from
Mrs. Louis Stevenson to Mrs. Sitwell that brought the
news.

During the first four of these six months at Honolulu
The Master of Ballantrae was finished, and in May
Stevenson wrote home, of Mr. Hole's illustrations : " Yes,
I think Hole has done finely; it will be one of the most
adequately illustrated books of our generation." In May
he paid a visit to the leper settlement where Father Damien
had laboured, on Molokai, a neighbouring island, "where
I can only say that the sight of so much courage, cheerfulness, and devotion strung me too high to mind the
infinite pity and horror of the sights."

In June Stevenson, his wife, and Lloyd Osbourne left
Honolulu in a trading schooner, bound for the Gilberts,
" the most primitively mannered of all the island groups

of the Western Pacific," and for the next six months were
lost to the ken of civilisation. The first letter to reach
England was one written to Sir Sidney Colvin in August,
and in it Stevenson spoke of his full intention of being
"home by June for the summer, or we shall know the
reason why." At the end of the year they " emerged,"
to use Sir Sidney Colvin's expression, in Samoa, where
Stevenson fell in love with place and people, stayed six
weeks, during them wrote his Polynesian story, *The Bottle
Imp*, and bought an estate on the side of the woody
mountain above Apia, intending to make of it only a
delightful place of " rest and call," but which was to be
his home until the end. For he was soon to "know the
reason why."

In February he left the fairyland of the Pacific, and
returned to Sydney,—to the streets and the civilisation he
hated. And here he was attacked by all his old symptoms,
mental and physical. He was overtaken by the same
chivalrous response to heroism, and quixotic defence of
the wronged, that had moved him to hatred of Gladstone
and shame of his country's shame at the death of Gordon,
and again to his mad wish to occupy the boycotted farm
and defend the womenfolk of the murdered Irishman,—
for it was the same hot-headed, righteously-indignant
Stevenson who, in these weeks at Sydney, penned the
Letter to Dr. Hyde (the harshness of which he afterwards
regretted), in defence of Father Damien. But alas, it
was also the same Stevenson physically, for he was once
again seriously ill,—fever and hæmorrhage as of old.
This decided him that he must settle for good on the
land he had bought at Samoa ; and : " I shall never
come back home except to die," he wrote.

So, from April till August 1890, instead of the journey
home, it was a journey in a steamer, the *Janet Nicoll*,
by a long route to the Gilberts and to other primitive
islands.

In August he again attempted Sydney, and was as a
result " bedridden " at the Union Club—Mrs. Louis
Stevenson in lodgings—and wrote to Henry James :

F

"I must tell you plainly—I can't tell Colvin—I do not think I shall come back to England more than once, and then it'll be to die . . . . Am I sorry ? I am sorry about seven or eight people in England, and one or two in the States. And outside of that I simply prefer Samoa. . . . I was never fond of towns, houses, society, or (it seems) civilisation. Nor yet it seems was I ever very fond of (what is technically called) God's green earth. The sea, islands, the islanders, the island life and climate, make and keep me truly happier." [1]

At the end of October, 1890, Robert Louis Stevenson and his wife returned to Samoa, to begin those last four years of his life—the final stage.

It has often been said that all the romance that hangs over the name of Prince Charlie,—the songs and the inspiration and the loyalty—is due to the fact that he lost Culloden, and left but a brilliant story and pathetic memory for Scotland to cherish.

How much of the romance that clings to the name of Stevenson—the thrill of hero-worship and the inspiration, and the almost personal love for him—is due to those last years of exile, to his vanishing from the ken of the civilised world into a sort of sunset glory in a far-off sky ? It was all so fantastic, so brilliant, so appealing to the imagination. Stevenson himself must have often felt it as a dream. Tho years of Pacific voyaging may have prepared him ; but it was not really until he settled at his own house at Samoa, and lived his life there, that the transformation scene was reached, and that Stevenson— the very troublesome Edinburgh boy, the careless Bohemian of Fontainebleau, the half-starving pariah of San Francisco, the indomitable invalid of Davos and Bournemouth,—woke in exile to find himself Lord and Master and Priest of a patriarchal home, chieftain of a devoted clan of feudal retainers, friend and adviser of Samoan dignitaries, an influence in local politics and government, and amazed no less by his own recovered health, and the active life it allowed him to lead, than by the four thousand a year that was the practical result of his

[1] *Letters.*

recognition as an author in Britain, in the Colonies. and in America.

Samoa consists of a group of islands, of which Upolu, a wooded island about forty-five miles long and eleven broad, is the most important. The property Stevenson had bought, and to which he gave the name of Vailima (Five Waters), was about 300 acres of virgin land 600 feet above sea level, and three miles inland from Apia, the chief town of Upolu.

When Louis Stevenson and his wife returned from Sydney to Vailima at the end of October (1890) they had to " rough it " for six months, living in a little four-roomed wooden house which had been built for them during their absence, waited on by one German servant, and superintending the work of clearing and planting, and then of building the permanent home. During this time they were often hard put to it to obtain supplies, because of the difficulty of transport over the roadless track from Apia.

From the time Stevenson settled in Samoa, he wrote monthly budgets home to Mr. Sidney Colvin, and these, first published as *Vailima Letters,* and now incorporated in the *Letters of Robert Louis Stevenson* (edited by Sir Sidney Colvin), are not only a record of his life there, but a vivid description of place, people, and events, and a study of his own character to the end. His Samoan hours during the first months were spent chiefly in the idyllic occupations of " weeding "—*i.e.* clearing the ground—and piping on his flute. He brought to this work of weeding all the energy and enthusiasm he expended on whatever his right hand found to do, and he loved it, and loved the physical weariness it brought, and neglected his writing to slink out and weed; and he described inimitably both the weeds and the weariness. But the labours on that wooded hill above Apia were broken into. During the spring Stevenson was not without interesting society, for Americans of note came to Samoa—Lafarge the artist, and Henry Adams the historian. And twice, early in the year, Stevenson went journeys. In February (1891) he went back to Sydney to meet his mother, who, in order to be with him, had left Scotland and all her ties there, and was cheerfully ready to face exile and begin life again among the incongruities of Samoa. Stevenson took his mother to Samoa, and she saw Vailima ; but the house not being ready to receive her, she returned to colonial civilisation till April. In March, Stevenson again left Vailima, going an excursion with the American Consul, Mr. Sewall, to Tutuila, a neighbouring island of the Samoan group ; but after this year he never made any more excursions, and saw very little even of his own island of Upolu, save his township of Apia, and the rides and walks round about Vailima. It was in the autumn of his first year at Vailima, 1891, that Stevenson began to take that active part in the troubled local politics which afterwards claimed so much of his time, and gave him so strong and unselfish an interest in life.

The Samoan islands had, since 1889, been governed under the Convention of Berlin by the three Powers— Britain, Germany, and the United States. When Stevenson went out, there were two kinsmen, Laupepa and Mataafa, and the Powers had made Laupepa king ; whilst Mataafa, his rival, lived in royal state in a camp close to Apia. The great rivalries far off of the three great Powers, and the small rivalries near at hand of the two native chiefs, were further complicated by the official incapacity of two men appointed under the Convention of Berlin and sent out in 1891, after Stevenson's arrival —a Swedish Chief Justice and a German President of Council. The conduct of these officials proved so dangerous for the peace and well-being of Samoa, that Stevenson used his pen in protest, and a series of letters from him began to appear in the *Times*, the first in 1891.[1]

So the last months of that first year at Samoa were divided between active outdoor life, politics, piping, and writing. Through the year he had worked laboriously

---

[1] These letters resulted in the ultimate recall of the two officials.

at his Letters on his Pacific Voyages for the *New York Sun* and *Black and White*, but the work, done to order, was uncongenial, and he gave it up. He wrote his South Sea story, *The Beach of Falesá*, and in November he finished *The Wrecker*, in collaboration with his stepson, Mr. Lloyd Osbourne, and then continued what Sir Sidney Colvin calls his " conscientious labours " on his History of Samoa, compiled out of the *Letters*, and of other collected materials ; but which he himself always said was to be reckoned as journalism, and not literature.

The beginning of 1892 found him busy, in spite of a sharp attack of influenza, seeing *The Wrecker* and *The Beach of Falesá* through the Press. He planned a novel of the South Seas, *Sophia Scarlet*, but it never was written. On February 13th he began *Catriona* (called, during the writing of it, *David Balfour*), fell in love, as did David, and as has every reader since, with both his heroines at once, and was so full of the pleasure and intense excitement of his creation, so wrapt in the atmosphere of home it recalled, that he wrote twelve chapters by March 9th, three more by the 15th, and finished the novel by May. In May—writing six or seven hours a day—he also finished his " conscientious " *Footnote to History*. He fully expected the publication of this, which showed up the mistakes of the government of the islands under the Berlin Treaty, might lead to his deportation. This indeed was a consummation devoutly wished, since his letters to the *Times*, by the two white officials ; and the expectation of this possibility lasted till the end of 1892. But when the book reached Samoa it gave no offence. The Tauchnitz edition, prepared for publication in Germany, was burnt by order of the German Government.

Meanwhile, life in Samoa was crowded with work and interests of all kinds. The patriarchal character of his home was established. " I am the head of a household of five whites and of twelve Samoans," he wrote to George Meredith. The whites were his mother, his wife, his stepdaughter Mrs. Strong and her small boy, and his stepson, Lloyd Osbourne.

During 1892 Graham Balfour, a cousin whom Stevenson had not hitherto met,[1] went out to Samoa and paid them a visit, and Stevenson and he became close friends. Another pleasant incident of the year was that Lady Jersey, with her daughter and brother, came from Australia to Samoa, to stay with friends. During their stay Stevenson took them, incognito and with elaborate precautions which much added to their enjoyment of the adventure, to pay a visit to Mataafa in his camp.

Towards the end of this year Stevenson yielded to persuasion, and added to and enlarged the house at Vailima. This outlay caused him some anxiety, because, though he was now earning a considerable income by his writing, yet the expenses of his patriarchal household, and all his kindnesses and hospitalities, swallowed all he could earn ; and the estate itself, Vailima, never paid, for nobody ran it on business lines.

Mr. Graham Balfour, in his *Life*, gives a pretty description of the last home of Stevenson. It was, he says, built of wood, painted dark green outside, the roof being of red corrugated iron with large tanks for catching the rain ; and on this iron roof the tropical rain fell with the noise of thunder. Round the house ran two broad verandas, one on the ground and one above, and on the upper one, boarded in, were Stevenson's study and his bedroom. In front was a lawn hedged round with scarlet flowers ; and here it was that they played tennis and croquet.

The chief feature in the house inside was the great hall, occupying the entire ground floor. From it rose the stair leading to the upper storey, its two posts guarded by two great gilded Burmese idols. Here, in this hall, were collected all the treasures that spoke of home and the past, —the furniture, not only from Skerryvore, of which Stevenson had been so proud, his first ownership, but the good solid respectable belongings from Heriot Row, that had seen so many old-fashioned Edinburgh dinners. And here Sir George Reid's portrait of Thomas Steven-

[1] Writer of the *Life of Robert Louis Stevenson*.

son hung, and here stood the marble bust of Robert
Stevenson.[1] In this hall the whole household met for
their meals, the fine damask and family silver and crystal,
partly also relics of Heriot Row, contrasting strangely
with the picturesque servants, in bronze semi-nakedness,
waiting at the table.

In this hall, also, Stevenson, after Mrs. Stevenson made
her home with them, used to have Family Prayers for the
household, at first every morning at eight, and later on
only on Sunday evenings, when all could assemble.   The
little service consisted of a hymn in Samoan, a chapter of
the Bible in English, Prayers in English, and then the
Lord's Prayer in Samoan.

Upstairs was the library, lined with books,—with
shelves devoted to Scottish history ; but Stevenson's
separation from books and libraries was almost as pathetic as his separation from friends,—the difficulty of
obtaining material and information for whatever he was
writing was a constant check upon him, and, in his
letters, each excited and delighted account of some new
literary project was soon followed by requests for books
he found necessary for it.   " Send me so-and-so," or " Is
there any book that would give me—," or "Did no one
write a diary or letters about the date of—,"—the call
comes again and again.   It was always responded to ;
but by the time the books reached Samoa, the inspiration
was gone, or other work had come in the way.   This
perhaps accounts for the numberless brilliant promises
that were never fulfilled,—the plans for work never begun
and the drafts left unfinished.

But the greatest wrench of exile was, of course, the
utter separation from his old friends,—old friends and
new, men and women, but, over and above all, from Mr.
Colvin.   It is pathetic how he urges everyone to come and
visit him at Samoa, and tries to persuade them of the
extreme shortness of the journey, and the ease with which
it can be undertaken.   And how often his heart took
the journey itself, back to the old haunts and scenes,—

[1] See page 7.

always to Scotland, to the glens and the mists,—to that
scholar-haunted quarter of London, the neighbourhood
of the British Museum, and to the door of "The Monu-
ment," as he always called Mr. Colvin's house there ;—
but most often to Edinburgh,—Edinburgh, where he had
been so miserable ; Edinburgh, that had slighted him
and nearly killed him ; Edinburgh, that he had so abused
and reviled ; Edinburgh, that he knew so well, and loved
and regretted so passionately.

The last two years of Stevenson's life were not altogether without their troubles. For one thing, his health
again proved itself unsatisfactory. He went in February
to Sydney, and he returned from Sydney not improved
in health. The spring was made anxious by Mrs. Louis
Stevenson being very ill ; and in the autumn the Samoan
war Stevenson had dreaded and had tried hard to prevent
broke out. Stevenson, always at heart a soldier,—as in
the days of his tin soldiers in the Colinton Manse, and of
the great and highly scientific campaigns in the loft of
the Davos chalet,—was stirred through all his being by
this, his first contact with real war.

"It is dreadful to think that I must sit apart here and do
nothing . . . and men sitting with Winchesters in my mind's
eye. . . . Do you appreciate the height and breadth of my
temptation ? that I have about nine miles to ride, and I can
become a general officer ? . . . "[1]

Stevenson had the chagrin and grief of seeing Mataafa
worsted and banished, and the Mataafa Chiefs, who were
his friends, cast into prison. He was active in helping
the wounded—got together a Committee, and turned the
Public Hall into a hospital ; and his kindness to the im-
prisoned Chiefs, his generous sympathy and tenderness
and understanding, showed his own character at its finest
and most unselfish in these last years, and brought him
a rich reward in the gratitude and devotion of the Chiefs.

After the war, in September, Stevenson again left
home for the sake of his health, —a voyage to Honolulu
this time. There, in a week, he broke down, and was

[1] *Letters.*

very ill with pneumonia ; Mrs. Louis Stevenson came to
him, and it was November before they were able to
make the voyage back to Samoa.

Illness Stevenson was accustomed to endure with
wonderful moral courage and invincible cheerfulness ;
but at last this bright, buoyant spirit of his showed signs
—at least in his letters—of giving way. What depressed
him was the realisation that his power of producing
imaginative literature was flagging. A year or so before
he had been attacked by writer's cramp, and although,
from that time, his stepdaughter Mrs. Strong had acted
devotedly as his amanuensis, he had had to adjust his
genius to the new method,—to dictate his teeming
fancies instead of penning them himself. This may have
helped to the difficulty he felt. But in fact the old
joyous ease and power of the artist seemed to be leaving
him. *The Ebb Tide* was composed heavily and with
effort, page by page ; and, though he was able to get
on with his *Family of Engineers*, he felt he could not
tackle the novels he had planned. All this preyed on
his spirits. The big new house had cost a great deal of
money, and poor Stevenson, who ought never to have
had to think of money, and who had had to think of it
all his life, was now, in spite of hard work (for the last
twenty years of his life he had written at the rate of
nearly four hundred pages a year) and of the income it
was now bringing him, harping on the thought of what
would be the financial effect if he were to lose his power
of writing romance, and how his wife, and her family,
would be left provided for.

The next year, the last year of his life, began with
happiness and gratification, for on New Year's Day, 1894,
he wrote to thank his old friend Charles Baxter, who had
long acted as his business adviser and agent, for his
scheme of the " Edinburgh Edition " of his works. In
May, when the scheme was matured, he wrote again to
him :—

" My dear fellow, I wish to assure you of the greatness of the
pleasure that this Edinburgh Edition gives me. I suppose it

was your idea to give it that name. No other would have
affected me in the same manner. Do you remember how many
years ago . . . one night when I communicated to you certain
intimations of early death and aspirations after fame? . . .
If anyone at that moment could have shown me the Edinburgh
Edition, I suppose I should have died. It is with gratitude and
wonder that I consider 'the way in which I have been led.'
Could a more preposterous idea have occurred to us in those
days when we used to search our pockets for coppers, too often
in vain, and combine forces to produce the threepenny necessary
for two glasses of beer, or wander down the Lothian Road
without any, than that I should be strong and well at the age of
forty-three in the island of Upolu, and that you should be at
home bringing out the Edinburgh Edition?"[1]

"By the early autumn," Sir Sidney Colvin states,
"the financial success of the scheme was fully assured
and made known to him by cable; but he did not seem
altogether to realise the full measure of relief from money
anxieties which the assurance was meant to convey
to him."

The last year was made happy to the exile also in other
ways. It was full of pleasant social life,—Mr. Graham
Balfour returned for another visit, bringing with him all
the talk of home and of those left at home. Other new
friends came; and to the officers of H.M.S. *Curaçoa* the
household of Vailima must have proved a veritable god-
send, as were they to it. In October there was the pre-
sentation to Tusitala of "Alo Loto Alofa," "The Road
of the Loving Heart"—a road from Apia to Vailima, the
whole labour and cost of which had been borne by the
Mataafa Chiefs, as soon as they were released from prison,
in gratitude to Stevenson for his constant kindness to
them.

But all this—the Edinburgh Edition, the cabled news
of his wealth, the devotion of the Chiefs, the literary
recognition from home, the cheerfulness of his daily life—
all this would not have been enough to let Stevenson
know before he died the highest reach of happiness, had
he gone to the grave with the feeling oppressing him that
his power had departed from him, that he could no

[1] *Letters.*

longer plan and carry out the work he had set himself to
do on earth, that the best in him was dead before him.
But he was spared this.

St. Ives, begun as an alleviation to sickness in January
of 1893, had been taken up again, and the dictating of it
had afforded him amusement at first, and then the book
began to flag and disappointed him.

"It *will not* come together, and I must live, and my family.
Were it not for my health, which made it impossible, I could
not find it in my heart to forgive myself that I did not stick
to an honest, commonplace trade when I was young, which
might have supported me during these ill years. . . . I did
take myself seriously as a workman of old, but my practice
has fallen off. . . ."[1]

In October he cast *St. Ives* aside, and set to work on
Weir of Hermiston, a book long planned, foretold in a
letter to J. M. Barrie as far back as November 1892, the
first chapter written in ten days with "incredible labour"
a month or so later, and "recast" in August 1893, but
whose subject-matter was always lurking in his mind,
especially when his thoughts were of home.   So, in these
last months of his life, he took up *Weir of Hermiston*
again.   And what happened ?   The creative power came
back to him, the thrill of inspiration ; and once again he
found himself writing easily and with all his old joy in his
sense of mastery.   The unfinished book, of all his books,
is, perhaps, Stevenson at his very best : so he judged it.
And, oh irony of Fate !—oh laughter of the gods !—the
book is of Edinburgh and the " lost forenoons " at
Parliament House, of old byegone debates at the " Spec,"
of Glencorse and the green Pentlands—the " hills of
Home "—and of all the perplexities of youth.   But it is
the writing of Tusitala, with not only the world between
him and Home, but with all his life between those days
and these.   So, with heart full of understanding and
human sympathy and charity begot of experience, he
wrote busily till Death came.

The death of Robert Louis Stevenson was the happiest

[1] *Letters.*

death imaginable. He had been writing his novel all the morning, and in the afternoon had been busy with home-letters from friends. It was the fourth of December, and the December budget to Mr. Colvin had not been begun, but was to be written next day. At sunset, Stevenson brought the last pages written of *Weir of Hermiston* downstairs, and read it to his wife, for her criticism. Presently, as they were standing together on the veranda, she with a sense of coming disaster, he talking brilliantly to re-assure her, he suddenly fell down at her feet.

He was carried to the big hall, and there within two hours he died, peacefully unconscious to the end, sur-rounded by his family, the doctors who had been fetched, and the little devoted clan of Samoans—some of whom remained kneeling on one knee to be ready to spring up and help as they might be told. Stevenson's friend, the Rev. Mr. Clarke, came, and knelt and prayed by him to the last.

The Union Jack that flew over Vailima was brought and laid over him, and the Samoans passed in solemn procession, each kneeling and kissing his hand. The request of Sosimo, his body-servant, was granted, and all night the Roman Catholic Prayers for the Dead were recited, in Latin and Samoan.

The Samoan Chiefs came, and spread fine mats on him, till the Union Jack was hidden beneath them ; and they cut a path with their knives and axes up the forest-clad mountain where Stevenson had wished to be buried, and up this steep path the coffin was carried shoulder high by the brave Samoans. And there, on the flat narrow ledge of the summit, in a grave dug by the hands of those who loved him, he was laid to rest.

On his tomb is engraved his own requiem :—

> " Here he lies where he longed to be ;
> Home is the sailor, home from the sea,
> And the hunter home from the hill."

LIVES AND CRITICISMS OF
R. L. STEVENSON

MANY books and essays, biographic, critical, and reminiscent, have been written about Stevenson. Of these, the standard Life is *Life of Robert Louis Stevenson* (2 vols.) by Graham Balfour.

The published *Letters of Robert Louis Stevenson* (4 vols.) ed. by Sir Sidney Colvin, contain not only letters from Stevenson's childhood to his last days, but also inserted biographical chapters by the Editor : these *Letters* are the best source for the study of the life and character of R. L. Stevenson.

Shorter Lives of Stevenson are that by L. C. Cornford, in *Modern English Writers,* and that by Margaret Moyes Black, in *Famous Scots Series,* and the article on Stevenson in the *Dictionary of National Biography.*

Miss Eve Blantyre Simpson's *R. L. Stevenson's Edinburgh Days* gives a graphic account of him in his youth.

Among the literary criticisms of Stevenson may be specially mentioned *R. L. Stevenson, A Study,* by Mr. Arthur Balfour ; *Robert Louis Stevenson, An Essay,* by Walter Raleigh ; *R. L. Stevenson, An Appreciation,* by Lord Rosebery ; *Robert Louis Stevenson,* by Sir Leslie Stephen ; and *R. L. Stevenson* in Edmund Gosse's *Critical Kit-Kats.*

The Faith of Robert Louis Stevenson, by the Rev. John Kelman, D.D., is a very sympathetic study of his character and genius.

But the final account of the life of Stevenson must be awaited in the volume which Sir Sidney Colvin intends to give to him in a series of *Memories and Judgments,* projected, and hereafter to be written.

ROSALINE MASSON.

INDEX